Understanding Islam
from a Christian Perspective

Understanding Islam from a Christian Perspective

Rosemary Sookhdeo

Isaac Publishing
McLean, VA

Isaac Publishing
6729 Curran Street
McLean, VA 22101
Website: www.isaac-publishing.com

Understanding Islam from a Christian Perspective
Copyright© 2019 by Rosemary Sookhdeo

All Scripture quotations, unless otherwise indicated, are taken
from the Holy Bible, New International Version®, NIV®.
Copyright© 1973, 1978, 1984, 2011 by Biblica, Inc.™ Used by
permission of Zondervan. All rights reserved worldwide.
www.zondervan.com The "NIV" and "New International
Version" are trademarks registered in the United States Patent
and Trademark Office by Biblica, Inc.™

All quotations from the Quran unless otherwise stated are from
the Quran are from 'Abdullah Yusuf 'Ali, *The Meaning of the
Holy Qur'an*. Beltsville, MD: Amana Publications, 1999.

ISBN: 978-1-7321952-2-6
Library of Congress Control Number: 2018962823

Cover illustration: "Grand Mosque (Djami Kebir), Larnaca".
Photo by Rosemary Sookhdeo.

Interior design and layout by Words Plus Design

Printed in the United States of America

Contents

Introduction

The triumph of Islam in the East in the seventh century A.D. was regarded by many as the judgement of God upon a degenerate Christianity and likened it to "Assyria the rod of my anger".[1] Today many Christians think Islam is very similar to Christianity and it doesn't matter which religion they follow, as all ways will eventually lead to God or in other words we are all on the same spiritual path.

One challenge that does face us, however, is – how much do we understand of the religion of Islam? Do we realise that Islam is more than a religion – it is a political system, a system of law, a cultural system and a religion all rolled into one. This comprehensive system could actually be called an ideology, which makes it different from other religions including Christianity.

As our Muslim populations increase and we interact with them in our daily lives, it becomes increasingly important that we can understand them as people but more important the religion of Islam itself. We are increasingly meeting Muslims in our everyday life in the workplace, in the universities and colleges and some have them as next door neighbours.

Many Christians are under the misconception that Islam and Christianity are very similar when they hear that the Quran mentions Adam and Eve, Noah, Abraham, the prophets and with Jesus – his virgin birth, his sinless life, his miracles, his ascension to heaven and his coming again. This is why it has now become important to know about the religion of Islam especially in relation to our Christian faith.

The cross and the crescent

The Muslims find in the cross the very centre of their opposition to Christianity. But for us the cross is central to our faith and is the symbol of sacrificial love, redemption, mercy and compassion. Christ is the conqueror whose victories have always been won through loss, humiliation and suffering. The crescent has no deeply religious significance for the Muslim and was most likely adopted by Turkish Muslims after the fall of Constantinople in 1453.

The word "cross" does not appear in the Quran as the crucifixion of Christ is categorically denied and Muhammad had such a repugnance to the very form of the cross that he destroyed everything that was brought into his house with the cross on it.[2] Muslims believe that in the second coming of Christ (as a Muslim) one of the first things he will do will be to destroy all crosses or in other words eradicate Christianity.

The cross is a very powerful symbol in the Muslim world today. For example, Egyptian Christians tattoo the cross on their forearm to declare that they are Christians and suffer persecution because of it. Young girls wear a cross to Universities and Colleges and are failed their exams because of it. In Malaysia when a new church is built, it is unable to have a cross on it.

CHAPTER ONE

Before the Advent of Islam

The Age of Darkness

Muslims refer to period before the advent of Islam as the Age of Darkness or the Age of Ignorance (*jahiliyya*) Muslims usually portray Islam as evolving in a primitive community of desert Arabs. However, Islam had its cradle in a part of the world where an advanced civilization had percolated. The influences of Egypt, Babylonia and Byzantium had reached the Arabian Peninsula, albeit second-hand, as it was on the fringes of the civilised world.[3] Northern Arabia was difficult to travel through, produced no valuable goods, and hence was not worth conquering.

Muhammad saw his mission as bringing the tribes of Arabia from darkness to light. For Christians, the light had already come into the world hundreds of years before Muhammad. This light was not limited to the Arabs, but was the "light of all people" (John 1:4). The light was Jesus the Messiah whose mission was to bring people "out of darkness into his wonderful light" (1 Peter 2:9).

Islam is different to Christianity in that it is not set in time or history

Islam in contrast to Christianity is not set in time or history and its primary source document, the Quran is located in neither time nor place. Everything about Muhammad was written down 150-200 years after his death and again we have only Muslim sources with no outside verification. This is in glaring contrast to the first writings about Jesus from the pen of the Apostle Paul, which were written as early as 55 AD, a mere 20 years after his death and resurrection.

The Quran covers a period of 23 years in the early seventh century. However, there are no definite dates ascribed to any event in the Quran. There is also a marked absence of any place names. It is only from later tradition that we know when and where the various chapters were claimed to be revealed.

Geographically, the Quran makes no reference to current events outside of Arabia, with one notable exception. In *sura* 30:2 it mentions the defeat of the Byzantines by the Sassanids of Persia. This is the only instance of an allusion of a world historical event in the Quran outside of Arabia.[4] But even this is inaccurate as the Byzantines are called "the Romans" – an incorrect term for the predominantly Greek armies of Byzantium.

Christianity in comparison is set in time and place

In contrast the Old Testament is punctuated with geographical references. The countries surrounding Israel are repeatedly mentioned in various contexts such as wars, famines, kings, political alliances and prophetic utterances.

Luke's Gospel anticipates Jesus' ministry by naming dates, places and personalities. "In the fifteenth year of the reign of Tiberius Caesar – when Pontius Pilate was governor of Judea.

Herod tetrarch of Galilee, his brother Philip tetrarch of Iturea and Traconitis and Lysanias tetrarch of Abilene – during the high-priesthood of Annas and Caiaphas, the word of God came to John son of Zechariah in the desert" (Luke 3:1-2).

Paul's missionary journeys can be traced with meticulous precision both on contemporary and ancient maps. The history and geography of the Old and New Testaments is woven into the entire Biblical narrative.

Arabia in disarray before Muhammad

In the sixth century after Christ the Arabs were a divided people fragmented into various tribes and at constant war with each other. In Arabia there was no central government of any form but there were unwritten rules which the tribes adhered to. However, we do know that many of the Arabs were able to read and write, from over forty thousand graffiti and a number of inscriptions from this period.

At this time the Arabs were not recognised as a people

The inhabitants of the Arabian Peninsula had no collective name designated to them, either by themselves or by people from outside. The word "Arab" was used to distinguish the way of life of the nomads from that of the settled population.[5]

The religion of the Arabs before Muhammad

The Arabs who believed they were descended from Ishmael had originally been worshippers of God but over time they changed. Now a number of tribes in Arabia worshipped their own tribal deity whilst other tribes had fallen into idolatry and polytheism. Many tribes also believed in a supreme deity named Allah – Ta'ala or God most high and called upon this god particularly when making a vow or an invocation. There is a view that Muhammad was called to reawaken the people to the worship of the one true God of their ancestors.

The name "Allah" was used before Muhammad

We also know that the name Allah was used before Muhammad from the occurrence of personal names like 'Abd Allah and 'Ubayd Allah the latter was considered to be the owner of the *Kaba*.[6] Muhammad's father, who died before he was born, was called Abdu'llah or "servant of Allah". Muhammad had a nephew named Ubaidu'llah. The tribesmen even called the *Kaba* at Mecca, Baitu-llah or "House of Allah".

Many of the Arabian dwellers also referred to their tribal god as Ta'ala or God Most High, this title being very ancient. Ta'ala could have been a corruption of the word Allah. Those using the word Allah were conscious of a historical divine unity.

The most binding agreements between the different tribes were confirmed by oaths calling on the name of Allah (*Allah Allahumma*) also using the expression "enemy of God". *Allah* is a contraction of *Al Ilah*, which is a word used with slight variations in different Semitic languages for *God*, with a prefix of the definite article *Al*. One of the words in Hebrew for God is *El* or *Elohim*, which is itself borrowed from other ancient Near Eastern religions.

The Arabs were not very religious. What worship they offered were to deities named Wudd, Yauq, Hubal, Al-Lat, Al-Uzza and Al-Manah and through the latter three goddesses, they addressed Allah himself. They referred to these three goddesses as the "daughters of god". Most Arabians regarded Allah as the father of the three goddesses worshipped at Mecca. Therefore, Muhammad did not invent the word Allah. He borrowed a name for God that was already being used by his people.[7]

Some scholars believe that the word Allah in pre-Islamic Arabia is evidence of a pre-existing religion practiced by the tribes. This was the religion of Ishmael and Abraham.[8] Muslims claim that God called Muhammad to reawaken his people to the worship of the one true God of their ancestors, which they had corrupted by idolatry and polytheism.

Al-Azraqi, a Meccan chronicler, reports that in the pre-Islamic *Kaba* at Mecca, alongside the idols of the three goddesses, "there was a picture of Abraham as an old man and performing divination by the shaking of arrows, and a picture of Jesus son of Mary and his mother, and a picture of angels".

Muhammad insisted that God called him not to found a new religion but to recall the Arabs to the "Faith of Abraham".

Judaism in pre-Islamic Arabia

The book of Acts mentions Arabs among the various nationalities of Jews who had travelled to Jerusalem for the Jewish feast of Pentecost (Acts 2:11). By the beginning of the fifth century, Judaism had spread to the Himyaritic kingdom along the south-western coast of the Arabian peninsula, in what is today Yemen. The Jews occupied the city of Najran, to the east of Himyar on the border between Saudi Arabia and Yemen, when they defeated the Christians in ca. 520 AD.

The Hijaz or holy land of Islam, a geographical region that comprises most of the western part of modern-day Saudi Arabia, already had pockets of Arabs who had become Jews, living among its settled population in the towns and oases.

Jewish tribes in the area

Yathrib, later called Medina, housed three Jewish tribes – the Qurayza, the Qaynuqa and the Nadir – as well as several other

Jewish clans. Jewish tribes had also settled at Tema, to the east of the Hijaz and in the Khaybar oasis, half way between Tema and Yathrib. There is evidence for Jewish settlements at Dedan, Hegra and most other locations along the main trade routes of north-western Arabia. Caravans travelling from Mecca south to the Himyaritic kingdom in Yemen or north to the oases towns of the Hijaz were certain to encounter Judaism.

In fact, on arriving at Yathrib Muhammad is supposed to have ordered his secretary, Zaid, to learn the *kitab al-yahud* – the book of the Jews. Muslim tradition also tells us that many inhabitants of Arabia and entire Arabian tribes were Jewish before Muhammad's arrival. However, it gives us little information about them.

Muslims borrowed the Arabic word *salat* (prayer) from the Jewish language of Aramaic as well as some of the postures for prayer, particularly the facing towards Jerusalem while praying. The Jews most likely brought monotheism to the Arabian Peninsula.

Christianity in pre-Islamic Arabia

In 2014, researchers from a French-Saudi expedition discovered what could be the oldest texts written in the Arabic alphabet in the desert of southern Saudi Arabia. The dozen engravings were carved into the soft sandstone of the mountain passes around Bir Hima –about 100 kilometres north of the city of Najran. The oldest engraving was from the year 469 or 470 AD. It was marked with a large Christian cross. The same cross systematically appears on the other similar stelae dating more or less to the same period.[9]

During the rule of the Roman emperor Constantine, an Arab tribe called the Tanukh converted to a Trinitarian form of

Christianity. Later, the Ghassan tribe, became Monophysite Christians. On the north-eastern fringe of the Arabian desert, the strongest tribe of Lakhm, became Nestorian Christians. By the late sixth century, Christianity began to take hold in Mecca and Medina.[10] Conversions were even occurring in Mecca and Medina because of Christian influenced brought about by expanding trade.[11]

"In pre-Islamic Mecca and Medina, conversion to Christianity occurred individually, with each convert undergoing his own independent religious quest," notes Ghada Osman.[12] Mecca was exposed to Monophysite Christianity with Abyssinian, Egyptian and Syrian elements, while Nestorian Christianity influenced Medina. Monophysite Christians rejected the orthodox belief that Jesus had a human and a divine nature. They asserted that there was only one, divine nature in the person of Jesus Christ. Nestorianism, on the other hand, drew a wedge between the human and divine natures of Christ, insisting they existed as two persons sharing one body and were completely distinct and separate. Early Church Councils declared Monophysitism and Nestorianism as heretical forms of Christianity and rejected them.

However, though we can point to a number of individual converts in Mecca and Medina, Christianity lacked a strong church and community in these two cities. All the Christians were first generation converts. They were relatively isolated from each other. They also belonged to different factions that were in conflict over clashing doctrinal positions.

Christianity seemed incapable of penetrating Arab life

Christianity proved to be incapable of penetrating Arab life as it existed and of transforming it from within. In particular this was true of the tribes of Arabia, who were self-sufficient and did not feel the need of a new religion so resisted any fundamental change. The Christianity imported into the region was mostly heretical and lacked Biblical teaching as there were no Bible portions of Scripture translated into Arabic, and was also highly individualistic.

The tribes in north-western Arabia in general, viewed Christianity as being politically allied to the Christian Byzantine Empire. This is very similar today whereby Arabs and indeed the whole Muslim world see Christianity as being allied to what they perceive to be the Christian West. Arabs who had adopted Christianity did not see it as an allegiance to Jesus Christ but on the same level that they recognised and used gods of Arabian life. This explains why so many Christians abandoned their faith for Islam, when Arab leaders proclaimed a religion that was uniquely Arab.[13]

Muhammad borrows extensively from Christianity

We will see how Muhammad borrowed extensively from Christianity, while rejecting its fundamental doctrines. For example Muhammad adopted the practice of encircling a holy sanctuary, which was the custom of Christians following their Lenten fasting. Christians would encircle their churches seven times on Palm Sunday – this was the first practise of encircling a holy sanctuary.

It was before the advent of Islam at the end of the month of fasting that Muhammad would come down from Mount Hira – he first goes to the *Kaba* to offer thanks and later to the feast marking the close of the fasting. At the end of the fasting, he returns to circle the *Kaba* seven times.[14] Even today, Eastern Christians encircle their churches once a day for seven days during Holy Week.

Islam has borrowed from the ancient Arabs

In many matters, Islam borrowed from the ancient Arabs or Sabians. The term Sabian occurs four times in the Bible suggesting that the Sabians refer to certain people from the desert or from Egypt and Cush (Isaiah 45:14, Ezekiel 23:42, Job 1:15, Joel 3:8). The context of the word in the book of Job appears to be North Arabia.[15]

A source from the early fifth century mentions the Sabians as descendants of Abraham and Keturah who practise circumcision on the eighth day and offer sacrifice.[16] The Sabians are supposed to have been a semi-Christian sect. Others have identified them with the Mandaeans, whose religion represents a combination of Gnosticism and ancient Babylonian heathenism.

Many Islamic rites taken from the Sabians

The Quran mentions the Sabians along with the Jews, Christians and Zoroastrians, who are also called Magians (*sura* 22:17). Many Islamic rites and ceremonies are identical to those practised by the Sabians, long before the advent of Islam. The Sabians had seven fixed times of daily prayer, five of which correspond with that of the Muslims. The Muslims have two other times of prayer which are optional, making the seven times of prayer correspond with that of the Sabians. The Sabians fasted for 30 days each year and if the month of the new moon was a short one they shortened the fast to 29 days. The Islamic fast of Ramadan lasts 30 days. The Sabians observed the festival of Fitr or the breaking of the fast at the end of the month. They would fast from the fourth quarter of the night until the setting of the sun. They also used to honour the House of Mecca or the *Kaba*.[17]

The *Kaba* was a place of pilgrimage long before the time of Muhammad

The *Kaba* was a place of pilgrimage long before Muhammad. The people of Arabia called it the Temple of Mecca or the House of God. Diodorus Siculus (60 BC) referred to it as the temple that the Arabs specially honoured.[18]

According to Muslims, Abraham and his son Ishmael built the *Kaba*. There is no historical proof for this claim. Nevertheless, it illustrates the antiquity of the worship at this sanctuary.

The *Kaba* housed some three hundred and sixty idols, one of which was said to be a picture of the Virgin Mary and child. The chief idol was Hubal, most likely the deity Baal. Other idols were Al-Lat, Al-Uzza and Al-Manat (representing the Sun, the planet Venus and Fortune) and were considered to be the daughters of Allah.

Pagan worshippers before Islam conducted their rituals at the *Kaba*. These included the circling the *Kaba*, kissing the black stone, sacrificing sheep and camels and stoning the devil. They would wear the Ihram or the single garment which is still worn by present day pilgrims to run around the *Kaba*. Muhammad would have practised these pagan rituals as he grew up. The *Kaba* and the black stone would become the central point of the Hajj ritual.

The black stone

There are many legends regarding the black stone built into the wall of the *Kaba* predating Muhammad. One tradition says that the black stone descended from paradise and was originally pure white, but became black through the sins of humankind by people kissing it with ceremonially unclean lips. The kiss which the pious Muslim pilgrims bestow on it today is a survival of the old practice which was considered to be a form of worship in Arabia. We now know that the black stone is of meteoric origin.

The inhabitants of the Arabian Peninsula were following an ancient form of Semitic worship called Fetichism, or veneration of stones. This was an ancient and common practice. Ibn Ishaq, Muhammad's earliest biographer, said that the custom arose with the Arabs carrying stones from the *Kaba* when they travelled and worshipping them.

Muhammad's family had a special interest in the *Kaba*

The Quraysh tribe, from whom Muhammad descended, were the custodians of the *Kaba*. They added its wooden roof and dug out the black stone buried by the Ayyad tribe in the mountains of Mecca.[19] Muhammad's grandfather was responsible for re-digging the ancient well of Zamzam in the courtyard of the *Kaba* following a vision he had on three successive nights whilst sleeping.[20]

Muhammad's tribe and family would have benefited financially from maintaining the *Kaba* as a pilgrim shrine. Muhammad would have had vested family interests in continuing to maintain the pilgrimage and other rituals based around the *Kaba*.

We can come to the conclusion with evidence that so much of Islam was borrowed from pagans, Jews, Christians, and Sabians.

CHAPTER TWO

It All Began with
a Man Called Muhammad

Islam began with a man called Muhammad who was born in 570 AD, almost 600 years after the birth of Christ. He had a very unfortunate childhood as his father Abdullah died on a business trip to Medina when his mother Amina was seven months pregnant. This resulted in Muhammad being the first and only child of the marriage. On his father's death his mother was left with very little – a slave, five camels and a few sheep.

After some years as a widow, Amina sets out with her slave and the young Muhammad to visit the grave of her husband in Medina. It was on the way home that tragedy struck when she falls ill and dies, Muhammad became an orphan at the tender age of six. His elderly paternal grandfather now took charge as his guardian.

Muhammad had an unusual upbringing

Muhammad's grandfather was a very important man as he was the ruler of Mecca and the leader of the Quraysh tribe who traced their ancestry right back to Ishmael. He was also custodian of the *Kaba* with the black stone. He produced ten sons, his favourite being Abdullah, who was to become Muhammad's father. When it was time for Abdullah to marry, his father looked for an alliance with another clan and a matrilineal marriage was arranged for him with Amina.

In a matrilineal marriage, the custom was for the woman to remain with her own clan or extended family and the husband would visit her from time to time usually for a period of about three days. Any children born would belong to the woman's tribe. After Muhammad's father's death his mother Amina continued to look after him. When she died his paternal grandfather then became his guardian until his death two years later, when his paternal uncle the merchant Abu Talib took over. What is interesting here is that the family line passes from the mother to the father.

Muhammad spends his early childhood in the desert

From an early age Muhammad had a nurse from a nomadic clan called Halima weaning him in the remoteness of the desert. This was a custom of his tribe, the Quraysh, who believed that the pure air of the desert would be healthy for its children and they would grow strong. After two years Halima said that she thought the climate of Mecca would not suit Muhammad and so continued to look after him in the desert for another period of two years.

One day, Muhammad had a very strange thing happen to him – he experienced an unusual fit and went into a type of trance. Everyone was greatly troubled with this occurrence as they thought it was a sign that an evil spirit had possessed him. They immediately took Muhammad back to his mother. Eventually they felt that there was no cause for concern, so they took Muhammad back to the desert for another year.

Muhammad continued to have these strange physical trances, which later led him to believe that he was receiving divine revelations.

Muhammad comes into contact with the surrounding Christian communities

Initially Muhammad worked for his aging uncle Abu Talib travelling with him as a trader. Tradition says that he was noted for his honesty. It was said to be as a result of this characteristic that Khadija Bint Khuwaylid, a powerful and wealthy business-woman (who was later to become his wife), who employed him in her family business which was one of the largest in Arabia. In her employ, Muhammad began to travel extensively around Arabia, Syria and Palestine, importing spices and silks. On these visits, he encountered the Jewish and Christian communities established there.

Khadija proposes to him

Muhammad seems to have remained a bachelor longer than most, which was most likely because of his poverty. It was his future wife Khadija who initiated their marriage by proposing to him. She said she "asked for the hand of the Prophet" because she found in him the qualities she most appreciated in a man. Khadija was forty and Muhammad twenty-five, this age differ-ence was very unusual and against the prevailing culture of the day. The marriage lasted for twenty-five years until Khadija's death. Within a few days of Khadija's death, Muhammad had married again. This time it was a widow named Sauda. He went on to marry eleven wives after Khadija's death and sanctioned polygamy to legitimise his marriages.

His wife's fortune was one of the largest in Mecca

Khadija belonged to the Quraysh aristocracy and was a powerful woman with economic independence and enjoyed freedom in both her public and private life. She obtained her fortune, one of the biggest in Mecca, by her two marriages to wealthy Makhumite bankers. Both husbands died each leaving her with a child.

With her marriage to Muhammad she produced seven children (three boys and four girls). However only one girl survived, Fatima who went on to marry Ali, who became the fourth Caliph and was her father's first cousin.

Muhammad and Khadija had a Christian marriage ceremony

Khadija and Muhammad were cousins and had connections to a Meccan Christian group called Nosrania or Nazarene. The Nazarenes were the early Jewish believers of Jesus of Nazareth. They were related to another cousin, Waraqa, who was a monk and led the Nazarene Church of Mecca.

Even though Muhammad was from a different branch of the family from Khadija and Waraqa, all belonged to the Quraysh tribe and had a common ancestor named Qussayy. The Quran mentions this group as *Nasorani* (*sura* 2:62, 5:18). *Nasorani* was also a generic name given to Christians.

Waraqa officiated at the wedding of Khadija and Muhammad and made a Christian marriage covenant, which affirms that only the death of a partner can end the bond of marriage.[21] This was most likely why Muhammad remained monogamous during Khadija's lifetime. Khadija's control over Muhammad's allowance may have also been another contributing factor to his monogamy.

Khadija's wealth enabled him to be free to pursue his own life

By making such a good marriage Muhammad now had status and position by virtue of his wife and was able to pursue his own goals and desires. He was aware that no political or social achievement is reached without social backing. Khadija however, retained control of her own wealth giving Muhammad an allowance for the duration of her life and a slave, which later was to become his adopted son. It was her wealth that enabled him to be free to meditate and to go around preaching.

Muhammad's other wives

Muhammad's third and favourite wife was Aisha, the daughter of a close friend Abu Bakr and an early convert to Islam. Muhammad married her when she was six and consummated the marriage when she was nine years old, whilst "still playing with her dolls". Muhammad died in her arms when she was eighteen. After Muhammad's death, Aisha briefly took over political leadership with the authority of the community. She even led an army into the battlefield against Ali the fourth Caliph and many *hadiths* are credited to her.

Aisha and her co-wives began to observe the new customs of veiling and seclusion which foreshadowed the changes that Islam would effect upon Arabian women. Today the head-cover worn by Islamic women is generally referred to as the hijab; the burqa, on the other hand, provides the most comprehensive covering: including the face and feet. There are many other cultural variations on Muslim women's headgear and clothing. It may have been Muhammad's suspicion of Aisha's unfaithfulness that led to the changes for women within Islam. She had lived in a time of transition and her life reflected both the period of *jahiliya* and Islamic practice. Women having authority over the affairs of the community began declining with the advent of Islam.

Christian heresy in Arabia

The Nazarene group that Waraqa and a large number of his Quraysh tribesmen belonged to was considered to be one of the heretical Christian sects present in Arabia at that time. They followed Jesus the Messiah, who they considered to be a great prophet but rejected his divinity and some went even as far as questioning the crucifixion and resurrection. They believe he was only a man like all men and received his revelation after his baptism by John the Baptist. This heresy was called Ebionism.

Ramadan was a custom in place before the advent of Islam

The Nazarenes observed Ramadan or a month of fasting as one of their customs. The Quran corroborates this practice (*sura* 2:183): "O believers! Fasting is prescribed to you as it was prescribed to those coming before you". Worshippers would return from Mount Hira to the *Kaba*, circle it seven times and then go to the feast for the close of Ramadan.

Muhammad meditates on Mount Hira

Waraqa and Khadija began to see Muhammad's potential for leadership and started preparing him with continuous spiritual instruction. Every year, for one month, they began going together on retreats to Mount Hira (about three miles from Mecca) for prayer, meditation and fasting. They did this for fifteen years before Muhammad again began having his visions. In a sense, Muhammad was following in the footsteps of his grandfather Abd al-Muttalib and other tribesman, who practised asceticism and devotion and made this annual pilgrimage to Mount Hira.

On Mount Hira Muhammad claims to have seen the angel Gabriel

It was whilst Muhammad was meditating on Mount Hira that he fell into trances and it was during one of these periods that he claimed to have seen the angel Gabriel, whom he said gave him a message from God to humankind. However, at first he was unsure of whether his revelations were from God or Satan. It was his wife Khadija who convinced him they were from God. The message he received however was contrary to that of the Bible.

The Quran

Muslims believe that the Quran was given by the angel Gabriel to Muhammad word perfect from tablets of stone in heaven and is the final revelation of God to humankind. They claim it has superseded all other books and revelations and Muhammad is considered to be the final and greatest of the prophets. Jesus (or *Isa* to them) was merely another prophet.

Muhammad's followers collected his revelations over the years and compiled them about 150 years after his death to form the Quran.

There has been a lot of debate about the genuineness of Muhammad's experience in the cave and thus the authenticity of his prophet-hood. As Christians we do not believe that Muhammad had a visit from the angel Gabriel with a message from God as the message the angel gave was contrary to Biblical teaching and revelation. We believe that Jesus the Christ was the final revelation of God to mankind and He was more than a Prophet – He was the Son of God.

CHAPTER THREE

Where and When
Did Islam Actually Begin

It all began in Mecca

Arabia was in complete darkness until Islam brought widespread enlightenment-this is how Muslims typically portray the birth of Islam. The historical reality, however, is far more multifaceted. On the one hand, the desert inhabited by the Arabs had always hung on the fringes of the civilised world. On the other hand, the combined influences of advanced civilisations had percolated into the primitive community of desert Arabs, even though the Hijaz had never quite formed part of the great ancient civilisations. Thus, it is fair to say that Islam was born in the cradle of a convergence of advanced civilisations, even though the Arabs had experienced the great civilisations of Egypt, Babylon and Byzantium only second hand.

Arabia was sandwiched between the two superpowers of the day – Christian Byzantium to the West and the Zoroastrian Persian Empire to the East. Islam began in the busy metropolis of Mecca. This wealthy commercial town was located on the spice route half-way between the ports and the markets in the North. Its inhabitants were conversant with both Arab trades-man and Roman officials and had a wide knowledge of the world outside of Arabia.

A need for an Arab identity

In the sixth century after Christ, the Arabs were divided into various tribes and at constant war with each other. There was no central government of any form in Arabia. The tribes adhered to unwritten laws, each tribe worshipped its own tribal deity and a tribe that had discarded its god did not feel it had lost anything vital to life.[22]

The Arabs owed their primary identity to their individual tribes and not to their faith. They spoke "mutually intelligible forms of a common language" and shared a common language of poetry. "But this is to speak only of a vague linguistic, and perhaps cultural, identity, not of a political one as 'Arabs'. There is almost no evidence for the existence of a collective 'Arab' political identity before the Believers created their Empire," argues Donner.[23]

In fact, since the ninth century BC, various Middle Eastern peoples used words like "Arab" to describe nomads who were "distant outsiders" and did not belong to a specific ethnic group.[24] Even when the Quran mentions the "*a'rab*" – it under-stand it as nomads who were viewed with contempt – it never speaks of "Arabs as such."[25] "People only began to call *themselves* 'Arabs' and to use it as a means to express group solidarity after the dawn of Islam in the 7th century AD."[26]

Even more problematic was the reality that the "urban settle-ments of Mecca, Taif and Yathrib, which enjoyed an autonomous political life, included only a small segment of the Arab population, and far from inspiring a sense of Arab identity, represented a way of life that set them apart from the Bedouins."[27]

Success by creating an Arab identity

The seed for a unified Arab identity was sown early in the seventh century when an Arab prophet, Muhammad, revealed an Arabic Quran in an Arabic tongue and sparked off an Arab expansion from the depths of the Arabian Peninsula. Until Muhammad, there had not been the slightest indication that the Arabs were wanting to express their faith through an Arab medium.

However, the Jews and the Christians had their Scriptures, but the Arabs were a people without a Scripture and ripe for a charismatic leader. Muhammad was to unite them and provide them with a purpose, an identity and a Scripture. Hence, Islam's Scriptures in the language of the Arabs was not only a literary event, it was the focal element in a corporate identity, as leadership and discipleship proceeded from and through it. The Arabic Quran is the Scripture of the Arabs.[28]

The Arabs, in general, offered little resistance when one of their own people proclaimed and imposed an Arab monotheistic religion that related itself to the natural conditions of an Arab community.[29]

The Arab Scripture made the Arabs masters over the Aramaic-speaking Christians

The Arab Scripture was to make the Arabs masters of the settled Aramaic-speaking peoples of Syria and Mesopotamia. Aramaic had become the language of the Church of Mesopotamia and Syria and the liturgical and ecclesiastical language of Arab Christians.

By the turn of the sixth and seventh centuries, Aramaic had completely replaced Hebrew as a living language. With the advent of a new defining scriptural text, the Aramaic-speaking peoples changed over to the Arabic language in the same way they had abandoned their earlier language of Hebrew for Aramaic. However, they now spoke the Arabic defined by the Quran and the religion of Islam, which in turn opened the floodgates for the potential for vast swathes of non-Arabs to convert to Islam.[30]

Muhammad was motivated by social injustice and fraud

Socially, Muhammad won the hearts and minds of the Arab tribes by denouncing the social injustices prevalent in the busy, commercial city of Mecca with its corruption and sharp divisions between rich and poor. This could have led him to believe that he was called by God with a message calling his people to repent as the prophets of old. At the onset he did not appear to be the preacher of a new religion.[31]

How did Muhammad manage to succeed

His social background was a major factor in his success, and some historians say he succeeded simply because he was a Meccan. Another important factor was that he had been born into one of the leading families, though poor, of Mecca and marriage to the wealthy widow Khadija had given him position, power and authority. He was the right person at the right time at the right place with the right message for that time in history.

At first Muhammad recognised the authenticity of the Jewish and Christian faiths

Spiritually, Muhammad embedded himself as the prophet calling his people to the ancient faith of Abraham that they had already received centuries ago. At first, he recognised the authenticity of the Jewish and Christian faiths and considered himself to be a prophet in line with the Old Testament tradition of prophethood. He chose Jerusalem as the direction to face during praying and adopted several Jewish practices. Only when the Jews and Christians refused to recognise him as a genuine prophet, he began to assert the true nature of the revelation given to him.

He then claimed that Islam was a renewal of the religion given to Abraham and the prophets of old and accused both Jews and Christians of corrupting their Scriptures. In a dramatic move marking a radical break with Judaism, he changed the *qibla* (direction of prayer) from Jerusalem to the *Kaba* at Mecca. Muslims face Mecca and not Jerusalem when they pray today.

Initial Arab resistance to Islam

Islam's birth in Mecca was fraught with tension as most of the inhabitants initially rejected Muhammad's message of the one true God. His compatriots severely persecuted him. Some even believed him to be demon-possessed.

His first converts were members of his own family. They included his wife Khadija, his son-in-law and cousin Abu Talib, and his slave Zaid who became his adopted son. The first convert outside his family was a wealthy merchant Abu Bakr whose daughter Aisha was later to become Muhammad's favourite wife.

27

After 10 years, he had only about 50 followers. In the face of this persecution, Muhammad sent a few of his followers to the Christian kingdom of Abyssinia (Ethiopia) to seek asylum. He himself fled to Yathrib 200 miles in the North where he had received an invitation from a group of the inhabitants who had already met him and accepted his claims. Wearied by severe internal conflict he was welcomed there as leader, judge, and prophet. The Jews and Christians of Yathrib were then sympathetic to Muhammad's claims because of his emphasis on the unity of God and his condemnation of pagan idolatry.

The Muslim era begins with the flight to Yathrib

The Muslim era began on 20 June 622, when Muhammad escaped from persecution in Mecca to Yathrib. Muslims call this event the *hijra* ("flight" or "immigration"). Muhammad later changed the name of the place from Yathrib to Medina. The Muslim calendar begins from this date, and it is a lunar calendar with only 354 days in the year. As this is 11 days shorter than the solar year, the dates on which Muslim feasts fall will vary every year.

CHAPTER FOUR

How Should We View the Quran

The Quran is the holy book of Islam and is said to have existed eternally in heaven, in Arabic, on tablets of stone. Hence, Muslims regard Arabic as the language of heaven and Arabic speakers have a special prestige in the eyes of the Muslim world. Muslims believe that the Quran is the actual words of God dictated word by word to Muhammad in the last 23 years of his life by the angel Gabriel. Even though the Quran is translated into many languages today, translations of the Quran do not carry the same weight or authority as the original version in Arabic.

The structure of the Quran

The Quran is almost the same length as the New Testament and is divided into 114 *suras* or chapters. The *suras* are not arranged in historical or chronological order but roughly in order of length, starting with the longest and ending with the shortest. The exception to this is the first verse which is the

Islamic creed. Most of the earlier *suras* are at the end of the book and the later *suras* at the beginning.

Many people find the Quran very difficult to read, as it is not possible to pick it up and immediately understand it as we do the Bible. To understand the Quran it is necessary to know the context of the *sura* and when and where it was said to be revealed. Many verses in the Quran appear contradictory and this is resolved by the "Law of Abrogation", whereby some of the later revelations abrogate or cancel some of the earlier revelations. In *sura* 13:39 it says "Allah doth blot out or confirm what He pleaseth."

Every *sura* (except *sura* nine) begins with the heading *Bismillahir-Rahmanir-Rahim which means* "In the name of Allah, the Compassionate, the Merciful". These words are found not only repeatedly in the Quran, but are also engraved on buildings, found on letterheads, plaques in homes and recited by Muslims in various situations. This expression is known as "The Bismillah", and after the *shahada* are the most familiar expression in Muslim devotion.

The Quran is read in conjunction with the *hadiths*

The Quran is read in conjunction with the second sacred source text of Islam, the six authoritative *hadith* collections, which include thousands of Muhammad's sayings that were passed on by his companions and were collected from 275 to 350 years after his death. The way of life of Muhammad as recounted in the *hadith* is known as the *sunna* and is used as guidance for his followers.

The main Muslim prayer

The first *sura* of the Quran has only seven verses and is the main Muslim prayer and is used to commence every prayer and prostration. It is called the *Al Fatihah* and holds a place of importance similar to that of the *Lord's Prayer* in Christianity.

1. In the name of Allah, Most Gracious, Most Merciful.
2. Praise be to Allah, The Cherisher and Sustainer of the Worlds;
3. Most Gracious, Most Merciful;
4. Master of the Day of Judgement.
5. Thee do we worship, And Thine aid we seek.
6. Show us the straight way,
7. The way of those on whom Thou hast bestowed Thy Grace, Those whose (portion) is not wrath, and who go not astray.

Sura 1:7 refers to the Jews as those with whom Allah is angry and the Christians as those who have gone astray. Muhammad regarded this *sura* as the foremost of all the revelations he claimed to receive.[32]

Emphasis on recitation of the Quran

The word *al-Quran* means "the recitation" and the Quran calls Muslims to recite its verses in slow, measured, rhythmic tones (*sura* 73:4). Muslims believe that the ritual of regular reciting the Quran in Arabic merits favour with Allah. Muslims treat this ritual with reverence and go to great lengths to master the correct pronunciation of the words.

This pursuit has developed into a science known as the "knowledge of pronunciation". Before a recitation of the Quran, Muslims will recite the words, "I take refuge in Allah from Satan the stoned". These words are taken from a verse in the Quran which encourages such action (*sura* 16:98). The word *ar-rajim* or "the stoned" is a description the Quran gives to the devil as a result of Abraham's supposed act of stoning him when he sought to prevent Abraham from sacrificing his son.[33]

Rocking while praying was originally practised in Judaism

There is no merit in reciting a translation of the Quran in any other language except Arabic. In Quranic schools and Madrassas, many hours are given to the recitation of the Quran while pursuing a rocking movement. Some say that the rocking increases the concentration. Rocking while praying has historically been practised within Judaism and is justified by Psalm 35:10 which says "all my bones will speak" referring to the praise of Hashem. Also in Malachi 2:5 it reads "before my name he will bow". There could also be a simple explanation, several students might have needed to share the same book during the *Tefilah*, so they would alternate in the bowing down, to enable each one in turn to see the writings.

The Quran is eternal written on tablets in heaven

Muslims believe that the Quran in Arabic is the exact replica of tablets of stone eternally preserved in heaven and is the eternal word of God, which was with God from the very beginning. They take the first verse of John's Gospel, "In the beginning was the Word and the Word was with God and the Word was God", to mean that the literal words of the Quran were with God from the beginning. Therefore, they believe that the Quran was "uncreated" not only in its content but also in its language. They consider that this makes Arabic the divine language or the language of God.

They believe that it was revealed to Muhammad over a period of 23 years by the angel Gabriel word perfect from the tablets in heaven. The Quran was sent down on the *laylat al-qadr* (night of power), which is one of the last nights of Ramadan. On that night the angels descended with the Spirit, that is Gabriel by the permission of their Lord. (*sura* 97:1)

Muhammad believed that the Quran is the final revelation of God and has superseded all other Scriptures

Muslims believe that Muhammad preached the same message of impending judgement as the prophets of old before him (Adam, Abraham, Moses, David, John the Baptist, Jesus) and that the Quran, given to Muhammad, testifies to the authenticity of the *Tawrat* (the books of Moses and the prophets), the *Zabur* (Psalms of David) and the *Injil* (the Gospel) given to Jesus as originally revealed.

Muslims believe that the Quran is the final revelation of God to humankind and that it supersedes all earlier revelations, including the *Tawrat* and the *Injil*, (which they believe were corrupted by Jews and Christians), and that Muhammad is the final prophet or the "Seal of the Prophets". *Sura* 33:40 says "Muhammad is not the father of any of your men, but (he is) the messenger of Allah and the Seal of the Prophets. And Allah has full knowledge of all things."

Muhammad wanted the Jewish and Christian communities to accept him as a prophet

Muhammad tried to get the Jewish and Christian communities to accept his revelations but with no success. He emphasised to them that his revelations accepted their existing Scriptures (*sura* 35:31f) saying that before the Quran existed there was the

Book of Moses and the Christian Gospels. He tried to convince them the Quran now confirmed the Pentateuch (*sura* 6:155) and also the Christian Gospels (*sura* 2:40f) In (*sura* 42:14) it says we have our works and you have your works. Between you and me let there be no strife. God will make us all one and to Him we shall all return. Whatever book God had sent down prior to the Quran Muhammad was prepared to accept. It is very interesting to note that at this point Muhammad was willing to accept both the Jewish and Christian Scriptures.

Muhammad declares that Islam is now the only religion accepted by God

However later Muhammad declares that God had now sent an illumination (*sura* 3:2) saying "We believe in God and what has been sent down to us and to Abraham and Ishmael and Isaac and Jacob and the tribes and also to Jesus and the prophets. We make no difference between them. They all have been resigned to God. Yet he who desires any other religion than Islam, his religion shall never be accepted" (*sura* 3:84-85).

God has sent apostles not only to various nations but he has also given each age or time it's book (*sura* 13:38). Muhammad changes his position and now states that Islam is the only religion that is now accepted by God.

Muhammad believed the Quran superseded all other Scriptures

Muhammad now believed that the Quran had superseded all other Scriptures including the Bible and was the final revelation of God to mankind (*sura* 5:18). When Muhammad began to realise that his account of various historical Biblical stories was different from those of the Jews and Christians he comes out with the *sura* that Jews and Christians have corrupted their

Scriptures. This view is held to this day by the Muslim community and they produce lists where Christians have changed their Scriptures which are used in their *dawa* or missionary activities.

Christians do not claim that their Scriptures were actually written physically by God himself but by godly men who wrote inspired and directed by the Spirit of God. The exception is the Ten Commandments which were given to Moses on tablets of stone when He went up Mount Sinai. Also heaven was glimpsed by John in the book of Revelation.

Muslims believe in infallibility of the Quran

No-one is entitled to change the words of the Quran. If he does he will be punished. A critical analysis is not allowed because it is the error free authority on Islam and is infallible.

Only those who are ritually pure are able to touch the Quran. The Quran is carefully wrapped in a cloth and placed on a high position in the room. Muslims consider the actual book to be holy and should not be touched by infidels or non-Muslims but only by the purified ones that is Muslims. *sura* 85:20f.

The Bible is seen in a different light, the contents are holy not the actual book. We are to read it constantly, keep it with us and is God's word to us to be read and absorbed. It is to teach, encourage, convict, and bring us closer to God through the Lord Jesus Christ. It is a means whereby God speaks to us and enables us to know God and His ways.

The Lord's Prayer in Christianity

The first *sura* in Islam would be the equivalent of the Lord's Prayer in Christianity which was shown great respect at this time. At the end of the Lord's Prayer *amen* was pronounced, which meant "so be it".[34] Jesus used the word *amen* to affirm his own utterances, and not those of another person and this usage was adopted by the church. It was used in both the Old and New Testaments. Amen was used in Jewish sources and went from there to Christianity before the advent of Islam. *Amin* (Amen) found its way into the *hadith* from two to three hundred years after the death of Muhammad.

CHAPTER FIVE

The Sources of Islam

The Quran contains some of the same stories and people which are present in the Bible. However, it confuses and contradicts major facts and other details regarding people, places, and historical and chronological events. Muhammad, for example, lists the Old Testament patriarchs in the correct order, but when he comes to the prophets, he loses the correct chronological sequence. *Sura* 4:163 names Abraham, Ishmael, Isaac, Jacob and the Tribes, but then follows on with Jesus, Job, Jonah, Aaron, Solomon and David.

Muhammad's knowledge of Biblical stories was limited

Muhammad seems to know the historical events of the patriarchs from Noah to the sons of Jacob, but the great prophets of the Bible from the eighth century BC onwards are entirely absent. The prophetic lineage stops with Elijah and Elisha. It does not include Amos, Hosea, Isaiah and Jeremiah. Jonah is an exception. Whether the reason for their absence is deliberate or unconscious, it produces a view of history radically different from the Old Testament. Again, even though the Quran mentions Jesus and Mary, there is practically nothing of the teaching of the New Testament.

There is no question that as the Quran grew in bulk its knowledge of Biblical stories became somewhat more accurate and though this greater degree of accuracy may have at times been due to the prophets memory, it is more likely he sought opportunities to acquire more information.[35]

The legend of Bahira

The legend of the Christian monk Sergius Bahira's encounter with Muhammad is well known in both Christian and Muslim tradition. Since the eighth century AD, the Syriac communities have been orally circulating this tradition. The written texts that relate at length to the encounters of the monk with Muhammad originate in the ninth century. There are two Syriac and two Arabic versions. There is a longer Arabic version, which includes 40 verses from the Quran which Bahira confesses to have written for Muhammad. This would show that the Quran originated in Christian circles.

The story was also written in Armenian and Latin. The essential outline of the story of Bahira in the Christian sources remains basically the same although there are variations.

Different versions all tell the story of the monk recognising Muhammad as the final prophet, while Muhammad was still a boy. The monk sees a miraculous vision about Muhammad's head and finds the "Seal of Prophethood" between his shoulders, exactly as it is described in his texts. The story is meant to show that Christians acknowledged Muhammad's prophethood, and to prove the Muslim claim that Muhammad was predicted in the Bible.

According to the Christian version of the tradition the very first words that Bahira writes for the illiterate Muhammad is the Bismillah: "In the name of God, the Merciful, the Compassionate". Middle Eastern Christians told the story as a polemic to prove that Muhammad did not receive his message from God, but from a Christian monk who tried to convert the Arabs to the worship of One God. They were rebutting the claim that Muhammad was a prophet and that the Quran was revealed and it explained away the argument of the prophet's illiteracy.[36]

In the story, Bahira explains to Muhammad the times of prayer, and the instruction that worshippers should face east where the sun rises. Syrian Christians normally face east to pray. However, Muhammad later returns to Bahira saying that his people have refused to follow this practice. Bahira gives in and lets Muhammad change the rules under the pretence of a new revelation.[37]

In some verses, Bahira tries to establish a clear structure dealing with prayer, food laws and fasting, for the followers of Muhammad to follow. Here, Bahira identifies the Christian symbolism of his instructions. For example, the threefold aspects of prayer refer to the Trinity, while the four rivers of Paradise refer to the four gospels.[38]

Muhammad comes to Bahira, as his people do not believe he is a prophet if he does not show them a miracle. Bahira assures Muhammad that he will solve this problem. He writes, "Nothing prevented us from sending the signs but that the ancients cried lies to them" (*sura* 17:59). The Quran does not record any miracles as such. It also states that Muhammad did not work miracles and did not regard himself a miracle-worker.

The Bahira legend also contains anti-Christian material. For example, Bahira appears to deny Jesus' crucifixion in a text quoted in *sura* 4:157: "They have not killed him and they have not crucified him, but it only appears so to them". Bahira claims to have written this and adds: "I meant by this that Christ did not die in the substance of his divine nature".[39]

Traditional Jewish influences in the Quran

1. Abraham and Nimrod

The Quran contains a story of Abraham's deliverance from the fire, which Nimrod makes to destroy him. Abraham's father makes idols and gives them to Abraham to sell. Abraham goes around saying, "Who will buy what will injure him and will not benefit him". Abraham then challenges his father and his people about their error in worshipping the idols they had made. He calls them to worship the one true God, which they refuse to do. One day when all the people have left the city, Abraham destroys all the idols with an axe. He places his axe around its neck of the largest idol.

When Nimrod, the king, hears of this, he takes Abraham and throws him into a fire (*sura* 21:62-68). Allah then speaks to the fire, saying, "O Fire! Be thou cool, and (a means of) safety for Abraham" (*sura* 21:69). Abraham is delivered unharmed from the flames.

The story of Abraham in the fire has no parallel in the Bible. However, it is a remarkable reproduction of a story found in the *Midrash Rabbah*, a book of Jewish folklore. The parallels make it evident that Muhammad does not produce an account that he has read from the Bible, but a story he has heard orally from the Jews. He repeats the story many times in different parts of the Quran but nowhere does he narrate the complete story. It seems evident that Muhammad and his followers knew the story very well and the story was popular in Arabia before his time.[40]

The Quranic passages founded on a mistranslation of a Biblical verse

It is possible to trace the Quranic versions of the Nimrod-Abraham story to sources that have mistranslated a Biblical verse. The Jewish scribe Jonathan Ben Uzziel misquotes Genesis 15:7, in his Targum. In the original, the verse reads in the following manner. "I am the Lord who brought you out of Ur of the Chaldees". The word Ur is a Babylonian word for the city from which Abraham came and is mentioned in Genesis 11.31. However, the scribe misunderstands the word "Ur" as the Hebrew word "Or" – meaning "light" or in Aramaic meaning "fire." The scribe thus interprets the verse to mean, "I am the Lord who brought you from the *furnace of fire* of the Chaldees". On Genesis 11:28, the scribe offers the following commentary: 'When Nimrod cast Abraham into the furnace of fire, because he would not worship the idols, the fire was not given permission to hurt him.'

The entire story seems to have risen from a mistranslation leading to the misinterpretation of a single word and has no foundation in history or the original Biblical text. Muhammad has also confused the chronology of Abraham with that of Nimrod, who lived many generations before Abraham.[41] Similarly, Muhammad is in error about Abraham father's name who is named Terah in the Bible. However, the Quran calls him *Azar*, evidently el-Azar (*sura* 6:74), a derivation from the name Eliezer in Genesis 15:2. Eliezer is Abraham's servant and not his father. Muhammad has confused the name of Abraham's father with his servant.

It is somewhat difficult to understand how Muhammad gave enormous credence to such a fable and accorded it the status of a revelation from heaven.

2. Cain and Abel

The Quranic account of Cain and Abel contains elements from the Bible, the Midrash and the Mishna. The story begins with the sacrifices given by the two sons of Adam, who are not named in the Quran, though commentators call them Qabil and Habil (*sura* 5:30-35). As in the account in Genesis 4, one sacrifice is accepted, one is rejected, and Cain slays Abel. The Quran gives no indication why one of the sacrifices was accepted and one rejected.

Then, the Quran has a sequel not found in the Bible. After Cain kills Abel, he does not know what to do with the body. God intervenes and sends a raven who scratches the ground to show Cain how to hide the body or the shame of his brother (*sura* 5:34).

The last part of the story is borrowed from the *Pirke de-Rabbi Eliezer*, a writing from the Midrash which is a commentary of the Torah (Chapter 21). It reads, "Adam and his companion sat weeping and mourning for him (Abel) and did not know what to do with him, as burial was unknown to them. Then came a raven, whose companion was dead, took its body, scratched in the earth, and hid it before their eyes; then said to Adam, I shall do as this raven has done, and at once took Abel's corpse dug in the earth and hid it".[42]

A comparison of the Jewish legend with the Quranic story reveals only one variation. In the former, the raven taught Adam how to bury the body, whereas in the Quran the raven instructs Cain on the burial of his brother's body.[43]

Most likely, Muhammad knew of this story from his contact with the Jews of the Hijaz. The minor differences between the

Jewish narrative and the form it takes in the Quran are typical of those one would expect to find in the record of a man relying exclusively on hearsay and secondary sources because he could not read the books from which the Jews were quoting.[44]

Muhammad has also missed the theological significance of Abel's sacrifice of a lamb, which in later Christian theology would come to symbolise a sacrifice of atonement.

A misinterpretation of a Biblical verse

The Quran also inserts the following verse into the story: And God sent a raven which scratched the earth to show him how he should hide his brother's body. He said, "Woe is me! I am not able to be like this raven"; and he became one of those that repent. *For this cause we wrote unto the children of Israel that we who slayeth a soul – without having slain a soul or committed wickedness in the earth – shall be as if he had slain all mankind; and whosoever saveth a soul alive shall be as if he had saved all mankind* (sura 5:30, 35). The lines in italics make no sense in the context of the story. However, a reading of Mishna Sanhedrin 4:5 clarifies the meaning of the interpolated sentence.

"We find it said in the case of Cain who murdered his brother: The voice of thy brother's bloods crieth. It is not said here blood in the singular but *bloods* in the plural i.e. his own blood and the blood of his seed. Man was created single in order to show that to him who kills a single individual, it shall be reckoned that he has slain the whole race; but to him who preserves the life of a single individual it is counted that lie hath preserved the whole race." This section from the Targum is the connecting link between the two passages in the Quran. However, the Quran omits this link thus rendering the entire section unintelligible.

Analysing the Quranic passage in the light of parallel Biblical and Talmudic passages demonstrate the flawed nature of Muhammad's revelations. This "revelation" was nothing more than a distorted repetition of information coming to his ears, some of it Biblical, some of it from later Jewish commentaries and some of it mythical and fictitious.[45]

3. Difficulties with the story of Lot

In the Quran there is a short reference to the destruction of the cities of Sodom and Gomorrah (*sura* 26:160-175) Lot was delivered with his family except for "an old woman who lingered behind" (*suras* 26:171 and 37:135. In a later *sura* 27:54-58 the woman is now identified as his wife. At this stage there is no mention of the angels or heavenly messengers who came in human form to destroy the cities.

In *sura* 15:51-77 Abraham is now linked to the story of Sodom and Gomorrah (these cities are not mentioned by name) and the angels visit him to announce their purpose, as in the Bible (Genesis 18. 16-22) In the Quran when the angels come to Lot they immediately disclose their true identities as well as their purpose and tell him to leave by night with his household. After this the townsmen come to Lot to demand his guests and as in the Bible (Genesis 19.8). Lot offers them his daughters. This account is very similar to the Biblical account except that in the Bible the angels only make their identification and mission known after the altercation with the tribesmen, and only then commands them to leave with their family.

What the Quran says is not logical for in that case Lot would not have been afraid of being importuned and he would not have had to offer his daughters[46]. In *sura* 11 Muhammad finally gets it right. The disclosure of the identities of the angelic guests

44

and their purpose to deliver Lot and his family and destroy the cities is now rightly placed after the altercation with the townsmen. Now, the fears of Lot about the safety of his guests when the townsmen arrive, makes sense. This is now consistent with the Biblical narrative but different to the account in *sura* 15.

Muhammad does not deny having a human teacher but only insists that the teaching came down from heaven. Now on the supposition that Muhammad had such a teacher, he would naturally be connected with something which appears to be a fact, namely the growth in accuracy of the acquaintance with Old Testament stories observable in the Quran. In the passages just quoted there is no awareness of the connexion between Abraham and Lot. In these later passages there is mention of the connexion with Abraham. If there were only one or two instances of this sort of thing they could easily be explained away , but there are a great many and the Western critic finds it very difficult to resist the conclusion that Muhammad's knowledge of these stories was growing and therefore is getting more information from people who were familiar with them[47].

4. Mary, the mother of Jesus

Mary is the only woman named in the Quran and has a whole *sura* named after her, signifying her importance (*sura* 19). However, the Quran derives much of the teaching about her from apocryphal sources and not from the Bible.

The Quran contains several references to legends in the apocryphal gospels. This suggests that much of Muhammad's knowledge of Christianity was taken from these sources. The most commonly quoted example of this says that Mary was brought up in the Temple of Jerusalem where she was fed by angels. This tradition is found in the *Proto-evangelium of James the*

Less, an apocryphal work, as well as other apocryphal gospels found in Egypt.[48]

According to the Quran, the mother of Mary, a "woman of Imran", dedicated her child while it was still in the womb to the Temple Service, but was surprised when a girl was born (*sura* 3: 35-36). The Quran says that God accepted her dedication and that she was committed to the care of Zachariah, the father of John the Baptist and remained constantly in her *mihrab* or chamber in the temple (this word today refers to the niche in all mosques giving the direction of Mecca). Only Zachariah had access to her (*sura* 3:37). Although Mary's mother was not named, some of works of the *hadith* say that her name was Hannah.[49]

The same verse also says that Zachariah was astonished to find Mary always supplied with food even though she was shut up in her chamber. When he asked where it came from she answered that it was from the realm of God. These details are never mentioned in the Biblical accounts of Mary, but borrowed from the heretical work of *The Life of St James the Less*. Many other things are said about Jesus in the Quran derived from similar apocryphal works, which circulated in and around Arabia in Muhammad's time.[50]

It is clear that this verse has confused various passages in the Bible. Mary is confused with Elijah, the prophet who was confined to solitude and fed by ravens who brought food from above (1 Kings 17:6). Mary's supposed mother Hannah prayed for a child and promised to dedicate it to the worship and service of the House of God. Here, Mary is confused with Samuel, as it was his mother Hannah who prayed for a child, promised to devote him to the service of God and made a vow (1 Samuel 1:11). When Samuel was born, he was dedicated to the House of God. Samuel later anoints David King of Israel.

The Quran has confused Mary not only with Elijah and Samuel, but with Anna the prophetess. Anna whose Hebrew name was Hannah, remained in the Temple day and night, worshipping and fasting for many years (Luke 2:36-38). The story of Mary is a conflation of these two completely different stories in the Bible of the two women named Hannah (Anna) from the Old and New Testaments.

Mary is also confused with Miriam, the sister of Aaron. "When Jesus was born Mary's neighbours said to her 'Mary! Truly an amazing thing has thou brought! O Sister of Aaron! Thy father was not a man of evil, nor thy mother a woman unchaste!'" (*sura* 19:27-28). Muslims say that Mary had a brother called Aaron, but in the Quran the only one called Aaron is called the brother of Moses (*sura* 20:30). Muhammad has confused Mary the mother of Jesus, with Miriam the actual sister of Aaron who was the first high priest of Israel. This time, the confusion does not arise from an apocryphal text, but from Muhammad.

According to the Bible, "the name of Amram's wife was Jochebed, a descendant of Levi, who was born to the Levites in Egypt. To Amram she bore Aaron, Moses and their sister Miriam" (Numbers 26:59). The father of Aaron and Miriam was a man called Amran. In the Quran, this is the very name given to the father of Mary, the mother of Jesus. He is called Imran, the Arabic form of Amran. Mary is called the daughter of Imran (*sura* 66:12).

To the last he appears to have adhered to the habit of picking up information and then utilising it...Having heard a Mary mentioned in the story of Moses and another in the story of Jesus, it did not occur to him [Muhammad] to distinguish between them[51]. In Arabic, Mary and Miriam are both Maryam. This is the most likely cause of the confusion.[52]

Explaining the errors in the Quran

The many errors that occur in the Quran show that Muhammad received his information orally, and probably from men who had no great amount of book learning themselves.[53] It is certain that he did not read (whether he was illiterate or not) either the Scriptures of the Jews or their folklore contained in the Midrash and other Talmudic records. If he had been able to do, so he would not have confused the two as often he did.

Muhammad almost certainly obtained his knowledge through direct conversation or from other secondary sources from the Jewish communities settled in Medina and other parts of the Hijaz.[54] Many of the names he gives to the prophets are not in their original Hebrew form but a form found in the Greek texts of the Bible. The prophets Jonah and Elijah are *Yunus* and *Ilyas* in the Quran. The New Testament Greek forms are *Yunas* and *Elias*. The Quran gives the names of these prophets as well as patriarchs like Isaac or *Ishaq* in the Quran neither in their Hebrew or Arabic forms but in the corresponding Greek form. This is puzzling because Arabic is a Semitic language in many respects closely related to Hebrew, which is considerably different to Greek and the Quran claims to be an Arabic Quran and a revelation to the Arabs in plain unequivocal language.[55]

CHAPTER SIX

Islamic Beliefs and Practices

The word "Islam" means "submission" to God and to his will as revealed through Muhammad, and a Muslim is one who submits. Muslim apologists often claim that the word "Islam" comes from the Arabic word "salaam" or "peace," which has the Hebrew equivalent of "shalom." This is linguistically incorrect. There is no connection in meaning between "salaam" and "Islam" or peace and submission. These are two clearly distinct words with entirely unrelated meetings.

The five pillars of Islam

Muslims have a set of religious duties called "the five pillars of Islam". These are compulsory for every Muslim. In early Islam, there was a discussion as to whether *jihad* should be a sixth pillar. Today some Muslims do accept *jihad* as the sixth pillar of Islam.

The first pillar is the confession or the creed

The confession of faith is the first pillar of Islam and is called the *shahada*. It is "I bear witness that there is no god but God (Allah) and Muhammad is the messenger of God". The creed is simple and short.

Muslims repeat this creed in the daily succession of required prayers. It is the Islamic prayer of conversion. A non-Muslim who recites the creed in the presence of two witnesses, becomes a Muslim. In cases of forced conversion, the person is forced to recite the *shahada* and is then considered to have converted to Islam. When a baby is born, the *imam* recites this *shahada* in the baby's ear. The *shahada* is literally proclaimed from the rooftops in Muslim countries, as it is part of the *adhan* (call to prayer) by the *muezzin* from the minaret. The creed proclaimed from the rooftops is in effect a denial of the divine Sonship and deity of Christ.

The second pillar of Islam is prayer

The second pillar of Islam is prayer. Muslims pray five times a day, at set times, facing towards Mecca. These prayers are the dawn prayer before sunrise, the noon prayer, the late afternoon prayer, the prayer immediately after sunset and the prayer after nightfall. The Quran gives no details of these prayer times; they are prescribed by the *hadith*.

Prayer at a mosque is announced by the call to prayer from high on the minaret five times a day. The *muezzin* cries, "Allah is great. I confess there is no god but Allah. I testify that Muhammad is the Apostle of Allah. Come to prayer, come to do good (success)". Early in the morning, he calls, "Prayer is better than sleep. Allah is great..."

Ablutions or ceremonial washing before prayer

Before prayer, the Muslim must carry out a ritual of pre-scribed ceremonial washing or ablutions. There are rules for washing four parts of the body: the face, from the top of the fore-head to the chin and as far as each ear; the hands and arms, up to the elbows; a fourth part of the head is rubbed with the wet hand; and the feet, washed up to the ankles. Many Muslims believe that if any of these parts of the body are not washed, the ritual prayers will be of no value. The Muslim should also be sober and ritually pure from sexual pollution for God to accept his prayers.

After having performed the ablutions, the worshipper then proceeds to the recitation of the prescribed prayers, accompanied by ritual movements. He can do this in private or public, and it is common in some countries to see Muslim men saying their prayers on the street.

Prayers in a mosque

Apart from daily prayers, there are communal prayers on a Friday that all men are obliged to attend, and it is during this collective public worship that the *imam* delivers a sermon. In these Friday prayers, some mosques include prayers cursing Jews and Christians. Most mosques have a separate room for women to perform ablutions and pray. A very few progressive mosques accommodate women in the main congregation, but even then in a separate place from the men. However, not all mosques have places for women, and so they are required to pray at home.

Extemporary praying within Islam

Apart from the ritual prayers called *salat*, there is a tradition of spontaneous prayer called du'a that could be considered as more like extemporary praying. This is another form of calling upon God.

However, many of the *du'a* traditions are merely a repetition of prayers instituted by Muhammad. Mystical experiences are more common within the Sufi tradition, which developed after the death of Muhammad.

Prayer is not about a relationship with God

Islam does not expect worshippers to develop a relationship with God in prayer; it is more an act of obligatory duty. In Christianity, there is a wide diversity of prayer, from structured, liturgical prayer to more extemporary prayers. Prayer for the Christian is more than a series of ritual movements and set prayers as it is built on a personal relationship between the individual and God. Christian prayer is entry into the presence of God through Jesus Christ as the mediator. Christians can pray at any time and in any circumstance and have the confidence that God hears and answers. There are many types of prayer: personal prayer, intercessory prayer (for others), prayers of adoration, prayers for healing, and sacramental prayers, to name a few.

The third pillar is the giving of alms

Islam has two terms for almsgiving. *Zakat* refers to the legal obligation of every Muslim; *sadaqa* denotes the voluntary offerings made at *Eid-ul-fitr*, the annual festival at the end of Ramadan.

Every adult Muslim must give *zakat* in proportion to the property owned, as long as they have sufficient money for their own subsistence. In Sunni Islam, the rate is 2.5 percent. *Zakat* is given to the poor and needy, those in debt, travellers, those who administer the funds and recent converts to Islam. It can also be used for the "cause of Allah", a phrase that denotes *jihad* (among other things). In Islamic law, *zakat* is a tax incumbent upon all Muslims. As a tax, it requires a political structure to enforce it. The payment of *zakat* is essential for achieving Paradise and non-payment may lead to eternal damnation.

Zakat is not usually given to non-Muslims unless they display leanings toward Islam. One Muslim missionary practice in our day has been to offer aid both to needy Muslims and non-Muslims as a means to converting non-Muslims. This has worked in many poorer countries of Asia and Africa.

Muslim leaders have suggested a system of deducting *zakat* from the secular tax Muslims pay in non-Islamic countries on the basis that *zakat* is earmarked for social benefits and hence helpful to all citizens. However, it has been argued that this yet another method of introducing Islam into secular nations by stealth.

In addition to *zakat*, Muslims are invited to make freewill offerings or *sadaqa*, for Islam regards generosity highly. Muslims may give *sadaqa* to a *dhimmi* or "protected person" who has submitted to Islamic rule but has not converted from Judaism or Christianity to Islam. Although classed as protected people, *dhimmis* are treated as second-class citizens. They have suffered discrimination and oppression and are forced to pay a special tax called *jizya*.

Islam considers prayer and almsgiving to be inseparable and it is said that almsgiving seals prayer.

The fourth pillar of Islam is fasting

The fourth pillar of Islam is fasting or *sawm*. Fasting takes place during the month of Ramadan every year. This is the ninth month of the Muslim calendar and the time when Muslims believe that the angel Gabriel first revealed the Quran to Muhammad. Ramadan is announced when one trustworthy witness testifies before the authorities that the new moon has been sighted. A cloudy sky may therefore delay or prolong the fast.

Fasting is defined as abstinence from food and drink, smoking and sexual intercourse during the hours between sunrise and sunset. Some Muslims do not even swallow their saliva. During the month of Ramadan, the family gets up early, before the sun has risen, and has a large meal. After the sun has set the fast is broken, often with dates, and then there is exuberant feasting every night until very late. It is said that the joy of feasting increases every night and reaches its peak on the 30th day of Ramadan, which is the final day of the fast and is called the *Eid-ul-fitr*. There is more food consumed during the month of fasting than in any other month of the year.

Fasting is compulsory for the Muslim, except for young children and the mentally disabled. Those who are sick, travelling, pregnant, nursing mothers or having their period are able to postpone their fast to a later date. This change of daily habits demands a high measure of personal willpower and self-discipline, and is less difficult in countries where everyone is doing the same.

As with prayer, Christians have no prescribed way of fasting. It is still very much a ritual of the Eastern Church, where fasting takes place every Wednesday and Friday and is a vegan fast, in which no animal or fish products are eaten. Eastern Christians also fast during Lent for 40 days and on various other days throughout the year, where fasting is from food and drink for a period of time. The person is able to choose the length of time of their fast, but it is always followed by a Eucharist and then a vegan meal. It differs from Ramadan in that the period of time is longer and it is not followed by feasting but a simple meal.

The fifth pillar is the pilgrimage to Mecca

The fifth pillar of Islam is the *hajj* or pilgrimage to Mecca in Saudi Arabia, where Muslims perform the *hajj* rituals around the *Kaba*. This takes place in the twelfth month of the Muslim calendar. The pilgrimage is obligatory once in a lifetime for those who can afford it, some traditions permitting the sending of a substitute even posthumously.

This pilgrimage usually has a great effect on Muslims, and on returning they are religiously revived and consider themselves new men and women. They believe that they have had all their sins washed away and some even say that they have become "born anew".

Pilgrims walk around the *Kaba* seven times, touching and kissing the Black Stone built into its corner. Muslims believe that the Black Stone descended from heaven to Adam, but was lost after the Flood and was returned to Ibrahim when he was rebuilding the *Kaba* with Isma'il.

A Muslim who has visited Mecca is called a *hajji* and is highly respected by other Muslims. A woman may only perform *hajj* with her husband's permission. Even then, she must be under the protection of a guardian.

Subjecting Islamic beliefs and practices to a critical analysis is extremely difficult. The very core principle of submission demands uncritical acceptance of the Islamic system of theology and beliefs. Although there are Muslim scholars who talk about reforming Islam, they are condemned as apostates by other parts of the Muslim community. Those who are considered blasphemous, such as author Salman Rushdie, risk losing their lives.

CHAPTER SEVEN

Islam, Angels and Demonic Forces

It is essential to understand the Muslim attitude to the cross

Muslims do not believe that Jesus died on the cross or rose from the dead but think that he was raised to heaven alive without death. Thus the very central doctrines of the Christian faith are denied by Islam. To them Jesus is not the son of God but is just a mere man and a prophet of Allah, like the other prophets before him, who have all been superseded by Muhammad the final prophet.

The word "cross" does not appear in the Quran although related words such as "crucifixion" are found there. However, a denial of the crucifixion is hinted at in the *sura* 4:157: "They slew him not nor crucified him, but it appeared so unto them".

Muhammad had such a repugnance to the very form of the cross that he destroyed everything that was brought into his house with the cross on it.[56] The Muslim attitude to the cross is not just one of denial and neutrality, but one of intense hatred and opposition. I remember when travelling around Turkish Northern Cyprus coming across a church that was standing empty and derelict with the altar area desecrated, and in a shed at the back were all the crosses, smashed.

In Muslim eschatology Jesus will come again, but he will come as the Muslim Jesus or *Isa*. One of the first things *Isa* will do will be to destroy all crosses, or in other words eradicate Christianity from the earth. This opposition to the cross is very intense. We read in Colossians 2:15: "And having disarmed the powers and authorities, he made a public spectacle of them, triumphing over them by the cross".

The cross is the pivotal point of spiritual warfare

The cross is the pivotal point of spiritual warfare, as it is the place where Satan and all the demonic powers are defeated by the blood of Christ. This is why they have such a hatred for the cross. We see a similar hatred in Islam.

The cross is a very powerful symbol for Christians in the Muslim world today. It is the symbol that brings persecution and suffering to the Church. Egyptian Christians unashamedly tattoo the cross on their forearms to declare that they are Christians and suffer persecution because of it. Young girls wear a cross at universities and colleges and may sometimes be failed in their exams because of it. In Malaysia no new church is permitted to have a cross on it.

In the context of Islam we can see clearly what is meant by the offence of the cross as described in 1 Corinthians 1:18: "For the message of the cross is foolishness to those who are perishing, but to us who are being saved it is the power of God."

Folk Islam

In Islam we encounter a religion every aspect of which is laid out in detail, a religion that in its basic form is simple to understand and follow, with all its rules and regulations. However, there is another side to Islam, which remains hidden but is just as important. This is the world of folk Islam or the outworking of popular Islam in the lives of people, with its angels and demons, *jinn*, cursing and the evil eye. These are not questioned but are accepted as part of normal everyday life. In the West the question arises: do we actually believe that this realm of demons and spiritual powers exists? We certainly find it in the Bible.

Angels in Islam

Angels live in what Muslims consider to be the other world. In Islam there are seven heavens, which Muslims believe exist one above the other with the throne of God being above the highest heaven. The angels occupy places in all the heavens but are arranged in order of rank. They believe that the highest ranking angels are around the throne of God singing praises and interceding for humankind.

In Islam there are two angels called Harut and Marut who teach magic to people. The Quran teaches that magic powers were revealed by Allah to these two angels in Babylon. They were then sent down to earth by Allah to teach magic to humankind. When Harut and Marut reveal the magic to someone they are to warn the person that it will bring them no benefit, only disbelief and they are to harm no-one with it except by the permission of Allah (*sura* 2:102).

In Hebrews (1:14) angels are called "ministering spirits". They are essentially spiritual beings but can take on bodily form when God appoints them to special tasks. When the women

59

went to the tomb of Jesus early on the resurrection morning they saw there an angel in the form of a young man. We read in the Gospel of Mark (16:5) "As they entered the tomb, they saw a young man dressed in a white robe sitting on the right side."

Demons and evil spirits in Islam

In Islam there are categories of demons or evil spirits. There are *jinn* (which have the characteristics of demons) and more vicious evil spirits called Shaytans. As Christians we do not distinguish between types of demonic powers, as we believe that they are all emissaries of Satan.

The Quran says that *jinn* or *jinni* are beings that were created by Allah from a smokeless flame of fire before the creation of man (*sura* 55:15). Smokeless fire is the name for the tips of the flames which are considered to be the purest and best of the fire. The Quran goes on to say that both *jinn* and humans were created by Allah to serve him (*sura* 51:56) and that the Quran was sent for both of them.

Muslims believe that *jinn* are part of the spirit world somewhere between humans and angels, whose abode is within the human domain rather than the heavenly domain. The *jinn* have power and capabilities that are beyond those of humans but they share certain qualities with them such as intellect, freedom and the power to choose between true and false, right and wrong, good and evil.[57]

In the Quran *Iblis* was the first *jinn* recorded as disobedient (*sura* 18:50) *Iblis* is considered to be the proper name for Satan. In Islam angels were created by Allah from light and *jinn* were created from smokeless fire, and therefore these are their origins, as humans' origin (Muslims believe) is clay (*sura* 6:2). The throne of *Iblis* is considered to be on the sea, and it is from there he sends forth his armies of *jinn*. The nearer the *jinn* to him, the greater its sedition.

Jinn form an important component in folk Islam, and some illnesses, medical conditions and even death are attributed to them.

Jinn in relation to humankind

Where the Quran censures and curses the *Jinn* and mentions the punishment that Allah has prepared for them. The obligations of the *jinn* are not the same as the obligations of humans but they are bound by commands and prohibitions such as the halal and haram. According to the *hadith* there are three types of *Jinn*-one type consists of snakes and dogs, the second has wings and flies and the third travels about.

Jinn are considered to be invisible to humankind but are able to assume what forms and shapes they please and when their form becomes condensed they become visible. They appear most commonly in the shape of snakes, dogs, cats, scorpions and human beings and can be either good or evil.

If the *Jinn* are considered to be good they appear as very handsome men or very beautiful women. If evil they are horribly hideous. They are more often considered to be evil than good and they have different names according to their degree of evilness.

The Biblical origins of Satan and evil spirits

Scripture speaks of good and bad angels, of holy angels and those who sinned and did not keep their first position or position of authority (Jude 6). These fallen angels are now part of the demonic realm with Satan. Satan, who was known as Lucifer, was the chief amongst the angels created to have dominion over the earth and was called the "son of the morning" (Isaiah 14:12 KJV). He was the most beautiful of all the created beings in heaven and was covered with precious stones and gold (Ezekiel 28 11-19). However, his beauty caused him to become proud, and sin entered as he desired to be as God and to have the supreme authority. In Ezekiel 28:17 it says: "Your heart became proud on account of your beauty and you corrupted your wisdom because of your splendour. So I threw you to the earth."

When God cast Lucifer out of heaven with all his followers (the fallen angels) he became known as Satan, which in Hebrew means "opposer, adversary, enemy". The fallen angels form the army of Satan or the forces of darkness, whose aim is to destroy the works of God. They ceaselessly oppose God and strive to deflect his will.

Muslim attitudes towards dogs

In most schools of Islamic law dogs are classed as ritually unclean. This means that Muslims may not pray after being touched by a dog. If they happen to be touched by dog saliva they must wash the "affected" area seven times before being considered pure again. Muslims also believe that a dog could be *jinn*. All this explains the Muslims' attitude and fear towards dogs. They keep as far away from dogs as possible, and if they encounter one they will desperately try to ignore it and not to provoke it in any way, as they believe that otherwise *jinn* could possess them or afflict them with sickness or death.

The evil eye and envy

The concept of the evil eye in Islam is that both people and anything that is precious to them are vulnerable to hurt or destruction simply by a person's envy. This envy or jealousy comes through the eye and is seen as a tangible force. Muslims consider envy to be one of the evil forces of the unseen that can affect a person adversely and are the major cause of crises in their lives. Evil forces are considered to come from a person who envies seeks to injure the life of the other person. It is because the evil eye is conveyed by a look that it is so insidious. Muslims say, however, that the harmful rays come only from the envier in states of malice, but that everyone can have spiteful, grudging impulses from time to time.

How to receive *Baraka* or blessing

The opposite to the negative force of the evil eye is a positive magic force or blessing known as *Baraka*. It resides with saints or holy people, who are in various locations where people are able to visit them. This *Baraka* can also be with objects and is generally received by some form of touch.

For most Muslims saints and shrines play an important part in their view of life. There are both living and dead saints in the Muslim world. In India, Pakistan, Bangladesh and the continent of Africa it is mainly the dead saints that are venerated at shrines. Saints that are living (*pirs*) are visited by people for healing, intercession, guidance or to bestow *Baraka*. Alive or dead, saints are believed to possess great power. The kind of miracles (*karama*) attributed to them include raising the dead, walking on water, covering great distances in short times, healing, having knowledge of the future, guarding people or tribes and being in two places at one time. Shaykh Zuwayyid, one of several saints venerated among the Bedouin of Sinai, is reputed to have filled a food bowl simply by looking at it.

We see from all this that Muslims are bound by fear and superstition and their lives ruled by it. For them the spirit world is as real as the physical world. What they need is a release from it and to find a new freedom that comes only through knowing Christ.[58]

The Night of Power

In the *sura* 97:1-5. It reads: "We have indeed revealed this (message) in the Night of Power. And what will explain to thee what the Night of Power is? The Night of Power is better than a thousand months. Therein come down the angels and the Spirit by Allah's permission on every errand...this until the rise of Morn".

For every Muslim this is a very important night. The Night of Power occurs during Ramadan, and Muslims believe it to be the night that marked the beginning of the revelation of the Quran to Muhammad and his mission of delivering it to humankind. They believe that there was a descent of the angels, and that the Spirit (Gabriel) with the permission of their Lord carried the Quran. "Sunnis believe that it falls on one of the odd nights at the end of Ramadan – the 21st, 23rd, 25th, 27th or 29th – but customarily it is observed on the 27th. The Shi'ah regard it as the 19th, 21st or 23rd night, which the 23rd being the most important" according to Imtiaz Yusuf.[59] Muslims are advised to "consult your imam or Muslim centres in your area about this observance", when it comes to what date they should observe the Night of Power.[60]

It is a night, Muslims believe, when the heavens are open and Gabriel and the angels descend and pray for mercy for everyone they find in worship. Any duty, such as reciting the Quran, is better done on this night than in a thousand months. (A thousand months can be understood as a large number.) It is also a night when all previous sins can be forgiven. It is considered a night of safety from any wrongdoing or mischief, but it can be a night of much violence against Christians.

When a Muslim is born

I always think of Muslims as having Islam engrained on their soul. It all starts when a woman is pregnant. She will visit a holy man or *imam* and will be given verses of the Quran to drink. The verses are written in a special ink and then washed into a glass with water, which she drinks. When the baby is born the *imam* immediately visits the family and shouts the *shahada* (or conversion prayer) into the baby's ear: "There is no god but God and Muhammad is the messenger of God".

This act binds the baby to Islam by spiritual forces and ensures that there is continuity in the faith. When Muslims come to Christ they often say that this act of binding at birth has been a barrier to their accepting Christ. When a Muslim does come to Christ we will need to pray for them that they will be freed from the spiritual forces of Islam by the name and power of Christ. If this prayer for release is not made they often do not grow in the Christian faith as well as we would hope. In many parts of the world, when a Muslim comes to Christ this prayer is included as part of the prayer to receive Christ into their lives.

CHAPTER EIGHT

Theological Differences between Islam and Christianity

Some say that Christianity and Islam have much in common and that they are blood brothers. But on a close analysis the two religions are found to be poles apart; the divide between them is so great that it can never be bridged.

At the heart of the division is the person and work of Jesus Christ. The centre of the opposition between Islam and Christianity is the deity of Christ, his status as Son of God, his atoning death on the cross and his victorious resurrection from the dead. Muslims vehemently reject the historicity of Jesus' crucifixion, death and resurrection. Instead, they claim that Jesus was transported alive into heaven without passing through death. Thus, Islam denies and even distorts the most fundamental doctrines of the Christian faith.

Jesus to a Muslim is not the Son of God

Jesus, to a Muslim, is not the Son of God, but a mere man and a prophet of Allah like other prophets who preceded him. It is

Muhammad, the final prophet, who has superseded the other prophets and even Jesus. On the other hand, the Letter to the Hebrews makes precisely the opposite claim and proclaims the finality of Jesus over every preceding prophet and revelation. "In the past God spoke to our ancestors through the prophets at many times and in various ways, but in these last days he has spoken to us by his Son, whom he appointed heir of all things, and through whom also he made the universe" (Hebrew 1:1-2).

Islam rejects Jesus as the Christ

Islam rejects Jesus as the Christ. The word "Christ" comes from the Greek word *Christos*, which means the "Anointed One". It is a translation of the Hebrew word for Messiah. The Old Testament prepares Israel and the world for the coming of the Messiah – the one who would be specially anointed by God and sent by God to save the world. Islam's categorical repudiation of Jesus' claim to be God's Messiah is characterised as a lie in the First Letter of St John. "Who is the liar? It is whoever denies that Jesus is the Christ. Such a person is the antichrist – denying the Father and the Son" (1 John 2:22).

Islam rejects the Trinity as polytheism

The very mention of Jesus as the Son of God presupposes the doctrine of the Trinity and the Trinitarian nature of God. Islam condemns the Trinity and calls it blasphemy. Conversely, Christianity holds the Trinity to be a central pillar of the Christian faith and those who have not accepted this have historically been known as heretics.

The Quran asserts that God is one in several places in the Quran (e.g., *suras* 16:51, 44:8, 47:19, 112:1-4), and monotheism or *tawhid* is the foundational doctrine of Islam. Muslims assert that the doctrine of the Trinity compromises this monotheism and entails tri-theism. They insist that Christians worship three gods and thus commit the unforgivable sin of *shirk* – polytheism or associating partners with God. It is also the worst form of idolatry.

The verses in the Quran that address the doctrine of the Trinity

There are three main verses in the Quran directly addressing the doctrine of the Trinity. The verses come from *sura*s 4 and 5.

> Believe therefore in God and His Apostles, and say not, "Three" (*sura* 4:171).[61]

> They surely disbelieve who say: Lo! Allah is the Messiah, son of Mary. The Messiah (himself) said: O Children of Israel, worship Allah, my Lord and your Lord. Lo! Whoso ascribeth partners unto Allah, for him Allah hath forbidden Paradise. His abode is the Fire … They surely disbelieve who say: Lo! Allah is the third of three; when there is no God save the One God. If they desist not from so saying a painful doom will fall on those of them who disbelieve (*sura* 5:72-73).[62]

> They misbelieve who say, "Verily God is the third of three." … The Messiah, the son of Mary, is only a prophet … and his mother was a confessor, they both ate food (*sura* 5:77-79).[63]

> And when God shall say, "O Jesus son of Mary hast thou said unto mankind, 'Take me and my mother as two Gods besides God?'" (*sura* 5:116).[64]

From the above verses, it is clear that Mary, rather than the Holy Spirit, is included as the third person of the Trinity. Either Muhammad received distorted information about the Trinity from heretical Christian sects, or he himself confused the identity of the persons in the Trinity. Muhammad mistakenly thought that Christians believed that God had a physical relationship with Mary that resulted in the birth of Jesus. The first Muslims therefore believed that the Trinity was comprised of father, mother and child: God the father, Mary the mother and their son Jesus. The Quran also makes it explicit that Christians are unbelievers who will be doomed to Hell for believing in the Trinity.

It is because Muhammad fundamentally misunderstood and misrepresented the doctrine of the Trinity, that he taught that it was not possible for God to have a son.

Islam has a false understanding of the Trinity

Muhammad replaces the Holy Spirit with Mary, the mother of Jesus and assumes that Christians worship Mary. In the process, he dilutes the doctrine of the Holy Spirit and renders it ambiguous.

When Muhammad was asked about the Spirit, he could not give a clear answer. The Quran describes Jesus as the "Spirit of God" breathed into Mary (*sura* 66:12). It claims "To Jesus the son of Mary we gave clear (signs) and strengthened him with the Holy Spirit" (*sura* 2:253). The Quran also goes on to say that God strengthens all believers with his spirit: "He has written faith in their hearts and strengthened them with a spirit from Himself" (*sura* 58:22). Islam fails to identify the Holy Spirit or Spirit of God as a person of the Trinity.

The Bible does not mention the word "Trinity"

So how can Christians defend the notion of a Triune God? In the fourth century, St Augustine of Hippo attempted to demonstrate that the fundamental logic of the doctrine of the Trinity can be stated in seven statements:

1. The Father is God.
2. The Son is God.
3. The Holy Spirit is God.
4. The Father is not the Son.
5. The Son is not the Holy Spirit.
6. The Holy Spirit is not the Father.
7. There is only one God.

The Jewish creed affirms the oneness of God

The Jewish creed, the *Shema*, affirms the oneness of God. "Hear, O Israel: The Lord our God, the Lord is one" (Deuteronomy 6:4). Christians accept this creed and even recite it in the liturgical services of some Christian traditions. Indeed, the New Testament emphatically reiterates this Jewish Old Testament creed. When Jesus is asked to name the greatest commandment, he quotes the *Shema*: "The most important one," answered Jesus, "is this: 'Hear, O Israel: the Lord our God, the Lord is one'" (Mark 12:29). In his letter, James the brother of Jesus writes, "You believe that there is one God. Good! Even the demons believe that – and shudder" (James 2:19).

The early Christians were all monotheistic Jews. As they continued to worship the one God of Israel, they were faced with two historical events – the resurrection of Jesus and the descent of the Holy Spirit. First, they confronted with Jesus – his life, death and above all his resurrection. They recognised that there was something supremely divine about Jesus. Thomas the apostle fell at Jesus' feet and confessed him as "My Lord and my God!" (John 20:28). The Gospel of John went back to the beginning and located Jesus as the Word who existed with God from the very beginning. "In the beginning was the Word and the Word was with God and the Word was God" (John 1:1).

71

The doctrine of the Trinity which had already been articulated by the apostles was ratified at the Council of Nicaea (325 AD) and established at the Council of Constantinople (381 AD). The doctrine of the Trinity completely debunks the simplistic and superficial assumption that the Triune Christian God is the same God as the Allah of Islam. Muslims would find such a theological equivalence deeply offensive.

Islam rejects the doctrine of original sin

The Bible presents us with bad news and good news. The bad news is that "all have sinned and fall short of the glory of God" (Romans 3:23). We are not sinners because we sin. Rather, we sin because we are sinners. Our innate propensity to sin comes from the "original sin" committed by our ancestors Adam and Eve in the Garden of Eden. If there is no sin, there is no need for salvation and if we are not sinners, we do not need a Saviour.

In the Quran, Adam does not "fall" and Adam's sin has no consequences for the "fall of mankind" (*sura* 2:36). Adam and his wife do sin in Paradise, but they confess their sin and God shows them the straight path (*sura* 2:37), since they sinned in a manner that they said of themselves, "We have been unjust to ourselves" (*sura* 7:23).[65] Hence, because there is no "original sin," there is no need for a Saviour since "no bearer of burden shall bear the burden of another" (*sura* 39:7). When man forgets God's commands, strays from them, or obeys the "whispers" of Satan, who is mankind's "enemy" (*sura* 35:6), he commits a sinful act. "However, he is not basically lost as a result, nor is he fallen or separated from God. When he again remembers God's commandments and takes refuge in God, he is in the position to again do good".[66]

CHAPTER NINE

The Muslim Jesus

Jesus is called *Isa* in Islam. There are two main sources for the Muslim Jesus: the Quran gives a history of his life, while the *hadith* establishes his place in the Muslim understanding of the end times. Christians who engage in dialogue with Muslims sometimes argue that the *Isa* found in the Quran is essentially the same as the Jesus of the New Testament. However, all the evidence from the Quran, the *hadith* and the New Testament leads both Muslims and Christians to precisely the opposite conclusion. In fact, the *Isa* of Islam and the Jesus of Christianity are radically different and irreconcilable in their person and work. If *Isa* and Jesus shared the fundamental commonalities then either Islam or Christianity would have to rewrite and reinterpret all the theology and teachings of our faith.

Isa is only a prophet

Isa (the Muslim Jesus) is a great prophet in Islam, but he is a different person from the Jesus whom we know as the Son of

God. In the Quran, "Christ the son of Mary was no more than a Messenger; many were the messengers that passed away before him" (*sura* 5:75). There are 28 prophets in the Quran and Jesus is one of them. Six of these prophets receive special titles: Adam the Chosen of God, Noah the Prophet of God, Abraham the Friend of God, Moses the Converser with God, Jesus the Spirit of God and Muhammad the Apostle of God. Muhammad is called the last and Seal of the prophets. Jesus is considered to be the greatest of the prophets before Muhammad, yet he is human like the prophets of old and is superseded by Muhammad, the "Seal".[67]

In the Gospels Jesus is called a prophet by those who first hear his teaching (Mark 6:15, 8:28) and accepts this title when he says that a prophet is not without honour except in his own country (Mark 6:4, cf. Luke 13:33). However, the New Testament, apart from the above references, makes no explicit mention of Jesus using the title of prophet.

Parallels and differences between the Biblical Jesus and the Muslim *Isa*

The birth of *Isa*

The Quran states that a "spirit" appeared to Mary and promised her a son. Islamic tradition assumes this to have been the angel Gabriel. The messenger goes on to say that the child will be a sign not only for his own people but for all humanity. *Sura* 19:21 states: "We wish to appoint him as a sign unto men".

The Quran says that *Isa* was born of Mary, who was a virgin. Mary, as we have earlier seen, is mistakenly called Miriam the sister of Aaron and Moses whose father was Imran. There is no mention of Joseph in the Quran. In the Gospel of Luke, when Mary asks the angel Gabriel how is her conception possible since she is a virgin, the angel replies: "The Holy Spirit will come on you, and the power of the Most High will overshadow you. So the holy one to be born will be called the Son of God" (Luke 1:35).

The place where *Isa* was born is not clear, but the Quran states that he was born in a remote place under a palm tree. Straight away *Isa* comforts Mary in her pain and her fear of peoples' rejecting her. *Isa* then speaks from the cradle and says, "I am indeed a servant of Allah: he hath given me Revelation and made me a prophet" (*sura* 19:30-31).

However, there are stark differences between the virgin births in Christianity and Islam. The virgin birth in Islam was a divine sign but was not indicative of a special role or purpose. *Isa* was created out of the dust of the earth. The Bible says Jesus was born of God and "conceived of the Holy Spirit". The virgin birth was the indication of his role as Son of God.

Isa and miracles

According to the Quran *Isa* raised the dead and healed the blind and leprous and breathed life into clay birds. "I have come to you, with a Sign from your Lord, in that I make for you out of clay, as it were, the figure of a bird, and breathe into it, and it becomes a bird by Allah's leave: And I heal those born blind, and the lepers, and I quicken the dead, by Allah's leave; and I declare to you what ye eat, and what ye store in your houses. Surely therein is a Sign for you if ye did believe" (*sura* 3:49).

The story of Jesus creating a bird out of clay is reported in a number of apocryphal gospels. The *Infancy Gospel of Thomas* narrates: "This little child Jesus when he was five years old was playing at the ford of a brook…and having made soft clay, he fashioned thereof twelve sparrows. And it was the Sabbath when he did these things...Jesus clapped his hands together and cried out to the sparrows and said to them: Go! and the sparrows took their flight and went away chirping". According to this verse (in Arabic) *Isa* did God's work and bore God's attributes (e.g. creator), but he was able to perform miracles only with Allah's permission.

Isa was sinless

Muslims believe *Isa* was sinless, as in *sura* 19:19: "(the angel says) I am only a messenger from thy Lord, (To announce) to thee the gift of a holy son."

Isa was the only prophet mentioned in the Quran who had these three characteristics mentioned above.

Isa is the "Word of God" and "Spirit of God"

Isa is called "Word of God" and "Spirit of God" – the only prophet who is given these titles in the Quran (*sura* 4:171). "Christ Jesus the son of Mary was (no more than) a messenger of Allah, and His Word which he bestowed on Mary and a Spirit proceeding from Him." However, the Quran clarifies that *Isa* is only "a" word of God and not "the" Word of God (or the divine *logos* who was pre-existent with the Father at creation) as described in John 1:1, "In the beginning was the Word, and the Word was with God, and the Word was God".

Isa brought a gospel to humankind

Muslims believe that *Isa* brought a gospel called the *al-injil* and a law to humankind. However, this gospel bears no resemblance to the four Gospels in the New Testament or to the Gospel, which is the Good News of salvation through Christ alone. Since the Quran denies the crucifixion of Jesus, it eliminates any possibility of defining the Gospel as the belief that "Christ died for our sins according to the Scriptures, that he was buried, (and) that he was raised on the third day according to the Scriptures" (1 Corinthians 15:3-4).

The Muslim gospel mentions nothing of the life of *Isa* or any of his teachings. There is also no reference to any content from the book of Acts or any of the epistles of Paul, Peter, James or John. The message *"Isa"* gives is one confirming the message of earlier prophets. "We [Allah] sent Jesus the son of Mary, confirming the Torah that had come before him: We sent him the Gospel: therein was guidance and light. And confirmation of the Torah that had come before him: a guidance and an admonition to those who fear Allah. Let the People of the Gospel judge by what Allah hath revealed therein. If any do fail to judge by what Allah hath revealed, they are those who rebel" (*sura* 5:46-47).

The apostle Paul categorically rejects any other message as "a different gospel which is really no gospel at all". He emphatically makes clear that the Gospel of the Lord Jesus Christ is non-negotiable. "But even if we or an angel from heaven should preach a gospel other than the one we preached to you, let that person be eternally condemned! As we have already said, so now I say again: if anybody is preaching to you a gospel other than what you accepted, let that person be eternally condemned!" (Galatians 1: 8-9).

Isa was only human and the son of Mary

Muslims believe that *Isa* was a mere man like any other prophet, and that all of them have been superseded by Muhammad. *Isa* was created from dust and lived like other prophets or messengers sent by Allah before him. Hence, it is not surprising that the Quran repeatedly refers to Jesus as "son of

Mary". This title occurs 23 times in the Quran, 16 times as Jesus, son of Mary, and seven times as Son of Mary alone or with some other title. In marked contrast, the New Testament calls Jesus "Son of Mary" only once in the Gospel of Mark. "Is not this the carpenter, the son of Mary?" (Mark 6:3 KJV). The Islamic commentator M. Ali notes that "the epithet Ibn Maryam (Son of Mary) is added to show that he was a mortal like other prophets of God".[68]

"The use of the title Son of Mary, found only once in the Bible, was not taken up by the early church generally. A search in the orthodox Christian literature of the centuries after the Bible was written has found no trace of this title, though it is possible that it was used occasionally or obscurely. Even apocryphal and heretical works rarely use it", writes Parrinder.[69] The exceptions are the Arabic Infancy Gospel and the Syriac Infancy Gospel where the title "Son of Mary" occurs five times and 15 times respectively. Both these works were never accepted by orthodox Christians and entirely rejected by the Church.

Christians believe that even though Jesus was fully human, He was also fully God. He had a human body and exhibited normal human characteristics such as hunger and thirst and weariness. Both human and divine natures came together in one person. "...Christ Jesus... being in very nature God, did not consider equality with God something to be grasped, but made himself nothing, taking the very nature of a servant, being made in human likeness", the apostle Paul explains (Philippians 2:5-7).

Isa is the Messiah but not the Redeemer

Isa is called the Messiah in the Quran eleven times. However, the title is empty and meaningless, as it does not carry the Old Testament meaning of "Messiah" or its fulfilment in the Jesus of the New Testament, where it means "Anointed One" and "Redeemer" or "Deliverer". The Quran does not explain the title.

Isa is not the Son of God

Muslims deny the deity of *Isa* and therefore do not accept him as the Son of God. They quote *sura* 4:171 in the Quran: "O People of the Book! Commit no excesses in your religion: nor say of Allah aught but the truth. Christ Jesus the son of Mary was (no more than) a messenger of Allah, and His Word which he bestowed on Mary, and a Spirit proceeding from Him: so believe in Allah and His Messengers. Say not "Trinity" desist. It will be better for you: For Allah is One God: Glory be to Him: (Far Exalted is He) above having a son".

Muslims believe that *Isa* confirms this himself, and say the idea that Allah could have a child is blasphemous. "They do blaspheme who say: 'Allah is Christ the son of Mary'. But said 'Christ O Children of Israel! Worship Allah, my Lord and your Lord'. Whoever joins other gods with Allah – Allah will forbid him The Garden, and the Fire will be his abode. There will for the wrong doers be no one to help" *sura* 5:72.

The Quran has many passages denying that God has off-spring. The most famous is the short *sura* recited daily by Muslims. "Say: 'He is God, One; God, the eternal; he brought not forth, nor hath he been brought forth; Co-equal with him there hath never been any one'" (*sura* 112). Another *sura* confirms this: "That is Jesus, son of Mary – a statement of the truth concerning which they are in doubt. It is not for God to take to himself any offspring; glory be to him! When he decides a thing, he simply says 'Be!' and it is" (*sura* 19:35-36).[70]

Paramount in Islam is absolute monotheism or the unity of Allah (*tawhid*) in Islam and this is in direct opposition to the

79

Trinity and therefore the divine nature and Sonship of Jesus Christ. Muhammad believed the idea that Allah should have a son is a lie believed only by those that are ignorant. We read in (*sura* 18:4-5). "What they say is nothing but falsehood!"

Islam not only proclaims the unity of God but constantly attacks the Sonship of Christ at every level from its theology to its practice. Muslims consider the statement that "Jesus is the Son of God" to be blasphemous, and it will cause them to react sharply with great disgust (*sura* 19:88-92).

Christians believe that Jesus was the Son of God

As Christians we believe that Jesus was the Son of God, and we should not be fearful in proclaiming it to any religion that is out to destroy this crucial point of our faith. Jesus is the very cornerstone and centre of our faith. It is in Him that we put our trust.

Interestingly, Jesus never speaks of himself as the Son of God in the Gospels of Matthew, Mark and Luke. Other people call him the "Son of God" but Jesus prefers to refer to himself as the "Son of Man", drawing this title from Daniel 7:13, where it specifically refers to a divine figure coming down from heaven. John's Gospel and Paul's letters refer to Jesus as the "Son of God".

Jesus was a personal manifestation of the Godhead

His two titles, "Son of God" and the "Word", ensure that we understand Him as a personal manifestation of the Godhead, equal with the Father. He is an accurate expression of God's glory and person. Our Lord is not merely a likeness of the Father but of "one substance with the Father". He and the Father are one. He is described as the Word, the pre-existent Christ, in a unique relationship with the Father.

John 1:14 reads, "The Word became flesh and made his dwelling among us. We have seen his glory, the glory as of the One and Only who came from the Father, full of grace and truth."

Colossians 2:9 states very clearly, "For in Christ all the fullness of the Deity lives in bodily form, and you have been given fullness in Christ, who is the head over every power and authority."

The eternal nature of the Son of God

The Nicene Creed uses the term "begotten" not "made" to clarify Jesus' origin. This means that He was not created as the angels were. Here we have the eternal nature of the Sonship of Christ. He was the Son of God before time began. "No-one has ever seen God, but God the One and Only, who is at the Father's side, has made him known", writes John (John 1:18). Jesus himself prays in his High Priestly prayer, "And now, Father, glorify me in your presence with the glory I had with you before the world began" (John 17:5). Also in 1 John 4:9 we read: "This is how God showed his love among us: He sent his one and only Son into the world that we might live through him." In John 1:1, the terms "Logos" or "Word" and "only Son" are applied to the same person.

Isa was not crucified or raised from the dead

Only one verse in the Quran explicitly addresses Jesus' crucifixion, and even that verse is ambiguous as to whether Jesus suffered death by crucifixion or not. According to *sura* 4:157-158, "That they said (in boast), "We killed Christ Jesus the son of Mary, the Messenger of Allah" – But they killed him not, nor crucified him, but so it was made to appear to them, and those who differ therein are full of doubts, with no (certain) knowledge, but only conjecture to follow. For of a surety they killed him not – Nay Allah raised him up unto himself; and Allah is exalted in Power, Wise."

The traditional Muslim interpretation of this verse is that the Jews tried to kill Jesus but were unable to do so. Quranic translator Yusuf Ali explains in a footnote: "The Quranic teaching is that Christ was not crucified nor killed by the Jews, notwithstanding certain apparent circumstances which produced that illusion in the minds of some of his enemies[71]". Muhammad would have had no idea of the meaning of the crucifixion: that Jesus died on the cross to provide salvation so that a person's sins might be forgiven, reconciling us to God and giving us the assurance of eternal life.

A *hadith* says that God substituted someone else in Jesus' place who appeared to be Jesus. A detail of the story recounts Jesus hiding in a niche in a wall and one of his companions being killed in his place.[72] Instead of being crucified, they claim, Jesus was eventually taken up to heaven. It is not clear whom they believe God substituted, but there are many theories, such as Judas, one of the disciples, Simon of Cyrene, a criminal, etc. The so-called "Gospel of Barnabas"(see appendix) which is an Islamic apologetic document claims that Judas Iscariot was crucified in place of Jesus. The Ahmadiyya movement believes that Jesus survived the crucifixion, migrated to India and eventually died a natural death.

It is possible that the ancient Christian heresy of Docetism has influenced Islam. The Docetics believed that Jesus only "seemed" to be physical and to suffer in his body. His suffering was only an illusion. Such tendencies find echoes in some of the apocryphal gospels. According to the second century *Gospel of*

Peter, on the cross Jesus "was silent, since he felt no pain", and at the end "the Lord cried out, saying, "My power, my power, you have left me". And when he spoke he was taken up". The Biblical Gospels however emphatically affirm that Jesus "gave up his spirit" and died.

The *Acts of John*, about the middle of the second century, claims that Jesus appeared to John in a cave during the crucifixion and said, "John, unto the multitude below in Jerusalem I am being crucified and pierced with lances and reeds, and gall and vinegar is given me to drink. But unto thee I speak". And later it says, "Nothing, therefore of the things which they will say of me have I suffered...I was pierced, yet I was not smitten; hanged, and I was not hanged; that blood flowed from me, and it flowed not". The ambiguity as to whether Jesus was slain on the cross and died in these heretical and sectarian writings bears a close resemblance to the Quranic ambiguity regarding the crucifixion and death of Jesus, even though the Quran states explicitly only that the Jews did not kill Jesus.

Muslims view the crucifixion as a defeat. If they believed Jesus was crucified it would mean that he established no earthly kingdom and achieved no success; he would have no followers and no legacy. Muslims also see crucifixion – to be nailed to the cross – as worthy only of criminal, as a disgrace and not worthy of the honour of a prophet.

As Islam denies Jesus' crucifixion, so it also denies the resurrection.

Isa ascended into heaven

Even though the Quran denies *Isa* to be the Son of God, it does concede that *Isa* ascended into heaven. "Allah raised him up unto himself" (*sura* 4:158). In the context of this verse, it apparently makes this claim to support its own view of Jesus escaping his crucifixion. In another verse from the Quran, 'Behold! Allah said:"O Jesus!, I will take thee and raise thee to Myself and clear thee (of the falsehoods) of those who blaspheme; I will make those who follow thee superior to those who reject faith, to the Day of Resurrection: then shall ye all return unto me"' (*sura* 3:55). Here, God raises Jesus to heaven, but only after first causing him to die.

According to the Muslim commentator al-Tabari, Jesus did not die but ascended body and soul to heaven while someone else died in his place. Tabari reports a story from tradition recounting a day when Jesus was together with seventeen disciples and the Jews came to the house where they were gathered. The Jews were intent on killing him but Jesus' image was implanted on all his disciples. The Jews were bewildered and demanded, "Show us which one is Jesus or we will kill all of you". Jesus turned to the disciples and asked, "Which one of you will win paradise for his soul today?" The faithful disciple who answered Jesus' summons retained the image of his teacher, while the others immediately regained their original appearance. This faithful disciple went out to the Jews, who took him and crucified him, while God took Jesus into heaven.[73]

Isa will come again

One day *Isa* will come again (*sura* 43:61): "A Sign for the coming of the Hour of Judgement: therefore have no doubt about the Hour but follow ye Me: this is a Straight Way." In Islam the coming again of *Isa* will be one of the main signs of the last days. He is presented as an eschatological figure who has an important role to play in the end times.

Muslims believe that *Isa* will descend to earth to the *Isa* minaret of the large Umayyad Mosque in Damascus. This was originally the Christian Cathedral in Damascus, which was demolished and rebuilt as a mosque by a Muslim caliph in 709-715. *Isa* will come as a Muslim warrior to destroy Christianity and Judaism and will establish Islam as the only religion in the world. He will fight all its enemies (including the Antichrist *al-Dajjal*).

"Narrated Abu Hurayrah: The Prophet (peace be upon him) said: There is no prophet between me and him, that is *Isa* (peace be upon him). He will descend (to the earth). When you see him, recognise him: a man of medium height, reddish fair, wearing two light yellow garments, looking as if drops were falling down from his head though it will not be wet. He will fight the people for the cause of Islam. He will break the cross, kill swine, and abolish *jizya*. Allah will perish all religions except Islam. He will destroy the Antichrist and will live on earth for forty years and then he will die. The Muslims will pray over him."[74]

To "break the cross" means to destroy Christianity. Pigs are associated with Christians, as both Muslims and Jews consider them unclean, and the killing of the pigs also refers to the destruction of Christianity. Under Islamic law the humiliating poll-tax (*jizya*) is paid by subjugated Christians and Jews to protect them from *jihad*. The abolition of the poll-tax signifies the revival of *jihad* against Christians and Jews, who will face the choice of converting to Islam or being killed.

Isa will then marry, have children, die and be buried alongside Muhammad.

Jesus as the Son of God threatens Islamic theology

Jesus as the Son of God challenges the very basis of Allah and Islamic theology. The deity of Christ challenges the primary tenet of Islam, the absolute unity of Allah. If God has a son, Islam is in error, and that is why this idea has to be so adamantly denied.

Every Friday, Muslims recite Quran 112 during the service at the mosque: "Say, He is Allah the One and Only, Allah the Eternal, Absolute, He begetteth not, nor is He begotten and there is none like unto Him".

This is a polemic against the Christian confession that Jesus is the only-begotten Son of God. Constantly repeated, it is a denial of Jesus as the Son of God and of the Trinity. The Muslim call to prayer ("there is no god but Allah and Muhammad is the messenger of God") goes forth over the rooftops five times a day from the minaret and is a polemic against both the Sonship and deity of Christ and the Christian faith.

The Muslims have Islamised Jesus into their *Isa* and made him to be the forerunner of but subservient to Muhammad. But Christ cannot forever be robbed of his glory, since the Holy Spirit is the great vindicator of Jesus Christ (John 16:4-15). The Holy Spirit in Muslim polemic is attributed to the coming of Muhammad, yet in the New Testament text it is clear that the Holy Spirit is the third person in the Trinity and the Glorifier of Christ, the Son of the living God.

CHAPTER TEN

Sin, Salvation and End Times

Sin and Islam

Sin is seen in a completely different way in Islam from how it is seen in Christianity. In Islam there is no consciousness of sin in relation to a righteous God or of the seriousness of it in relation to faith. Islam rejects the doctrine of original sin and the account of Adam's fall and its consequences for the "fall of mankind".[75] The Quran teaches however, that human beings are not "fallen" or separated from God.[76]

Islam explains man's nature at birth as *fitrah* – a state of intrinsic goodness. Like Adam, people are born pure and sinless. "Every child is born in a state of *fitrah*, and social environment causes the individual to deviate from this state", writes Islamic scholar Yasien Mohamed.[77] This is very different from the Biblical teaching that we are "sinful from the time my mother conceived me" (Psalm 51:5) and "sin entered the world through one man, and death through sin, and in this way death came to all people, because all sinned" (Romans 5:12).

Islam does not conceive of sin in relation to a holy and righteous God. The missionary Samuel Zwemer points out how God's holiness is completely ignored in the Quran.[78] "If any one does evil or wrongs his own soul... And if any one earns sin, He earns it against His own soul: for Allah is full of knowledge and wisdom" (*sura* 4:110-111).

A Muslim will have no assurance of the forgiveness of sins

Sin is seen within the context of a legalistic framework as an act of wrongdoing and not specifically related to the human heart. Islam distinguishes between the greater and the lesser sins. Greater sins would include adultery, drinking alcohol, murder, homosexuality, false testimony and theft, amongst many others. Greater sins are more serious and will lead to punishment; the lesser sins are common to everyone and are much easier to be forgiven or overlooked. This breaking of the law can be remedied by good deeds.

To a Muslim the most serious sins would be:

1. The sin of *shirk*, associating someone else with Allah is an unpardonable sin. Christians commit this sin of *shirk*, by associating someone else with Allah, when they claim that Jesus is the Son of God.

2. The sin of apostasy or leaving the Muslim faith is so serious that Sharia prescribes the death penalty for a sane adult man and sometimes imprisonment for a woman until she repents. This can be the barrier to Muslims' coming to Christ and the fear of committing this can bind them to the religion of Islam.

3. Sins such as murder and adultery.

When we talk about Jesus taking our sin on himself on the cross and giving us forgiveness of sin when we accept him into our life this has little meaning for the Muslim. As Christians we consider ourselves to be sinful in that we constantly do things that are contrary to what God desires.

The gravity of sin in Islam is diluted by treating sin as failing to remember God's instructions, rather than rebellion against God as in Christianity.

The central Christian doctrine of the atonement, wherein our Lord Jesus takes upon himself the punishment for our sin and becomes a mediator for the human race, is absent in Islam. Muhammad plays no mediatory role in the Quran, as the following verses makes clear. "O ye who believe! Spend out of (the bounties). We have provided for you, before the Day comes when no bargaining (will avail), nor friendship nor intercession" (*sura* 2:254). In fact, according to a well-known *hadith*, Muhammad worried about future judgment on his own family. "O Safiyah, the Aunt of Allah's Apostle! I cannot save you from Allah's Punishment; O Fatima bint Muhammad [his daughter]! Ask me anything from my wealth, but I cannot save you from Allah's Punishment".[79]

The Quran leaves Muslims with little assurance of salvation, since Muhammad could not save even his own relatives. As Christians, "since we have been justified through faith, we have peace with God through our Lord Jesus Christ" (Romans 5:1) and we are assured of salvation because "there is now no condemnation for those who are in Christ Jesus" (Romans 8:1). Moreover, Jesus himself assures his followers of eternal life when he says, "I give them eternal life, and they shall never perish; no one can snatch them out of my hand" (John 10:28).

Salvation and Islam

Salvation as we know it in Christianity does not really exist within Islam. Even the word "salvation" has no equivalent in Islamic thought. In Christianity sin causes separation from a holy God, and our sins are forgiven or blotted out when we receive salvation by the acceptance of Jesus Christ as Lord and Saviour. We look to the cross and resurrection, to Jesus dying for our sins and rising again for our justification, and to the assurance we have of eternal life. In Christianity, there is an inextricable link between salvation and sin.

In contrast, Muslims understand the phrase "being saved" only in the context of being delivered from hell-fire to paradise, not in the context of sin's causing separation from God and the assurance of eternal life. Many converts from Islam say that the Christian concept of salvation was the very thing that attracted them to Christ.

In Islam there is no assurance of heaven

Islam does not make is clear whether a person will go to heaven and hell. Whilst some texts say that all Muslims will have to go through hell before entering paradise, others indicate that those who believe and do right – the god-fearing – will enter the Gardens of Delight or Paradise.[80] "*Jannah,* or Heaven, is the place where our soul is rewarded for listening to its *fitrah,* or inner nature", writes Yahiya Emerick.[81]

Here we see the linking of believing and doing good works. However, the assurance of one's eternal destiny and escape from the agony of hell-fire is lacking within Islam, and Muslims can only hope for Paradise but with no certainty. We need to share with Muslims that it is possible to have the assurance of heaven through putting our trust in Jesus Christ.

This can be a very effective point to share in evangelism as it shows up a weakness within Islam. Islam overcomes this weakness by teaching the assurance of salvation in the exceptional case of martyrdom. To fight for Islam or to engage in *jihad* is to be a testimony or *shahada*. The people who take part are called *shahids* (martyrs or witnesses), and their actions are recognised as self-sacrificing and noble. Martyrdom is not regarded as suicide or even related to it. Muslims believe that *shahids* will go immediately to Paradise with all their sins forgiven. This act can be the only assurance of heaven after death for the Muslim. The martyr can then intercede for seventy of his relatives to enter Paradise immediately on their death.

A Muslim woman's destiny in eternity

What happens when a Muslim woman dies? Does she face the same fate as her husband or is there an entirely different set of rules? What happens if a woman decides to become a martyr? One Muslim woman caught before she could blow herself up expected to become "the purest and most beautiful form of angel at the highest level possible in heaven".[82]

However, Muhammad looked into hell and saw that the majority of its inhabitants were women. Bukhari's *hadith* says, "Once Allah's Apostle said to a group of women, 'Give alms, as I have seen that the majority of the dwellers of Hell-fire were you (women).'"[83]

This *hadith* and a number of others state that the majority of the people in hell are women. So how does a woman get to Paradise? Elsewhere, the *hadith* teaches that a woman gets to Paradise by being absolutely obedient to her husband. It is this that shows her piety and guarantees her eternal destiny. He is her paradise or her hell, and without obedience to her husband, there is no heaven for a woman.

The wives of the righteous and obedient are mentioned as accompanying their husbands in Paradise. Women in Paradise must be submissive, subordinate, veiled and secluded in the harems of heaven, watching quietly as their husbands make love with the beautiful *houris* (perpetual virgins) of Paradise. Man is her master on earth and she will be subjugated to him forever in heaven as well. There is no provision made for single women in heaven.

In evangelism to Muslim women, talking about the assurance and hope of heaven can really speak to their hearts. If they remain within Islam, they have a depressing future with no hope before them when they die. We need to share how we have this eternal destiny with the Kings of Kings and Lord of Lords and they can have this glorious and eternal future in front of them as well. Many Muslim women come to Christ to find this assurance of salvation.

Judgement day for the Muslim

A Muslim can never be sure of his salvation at the Last Judgement. The first thing to be judged will be prayer. Failure to pray can render a Muslim an unbeliever and will result in his being thrown into the fires of hell. To avoid hell he must repent before he dies, but even then he can never be sure of his destiny. A Muslim who has fallen into unbelief, like the person who leaves Islam, will suffer the eternal fires of hell. Those who have committed minor sins and have not repented will, after a period in hell, be able to enter paradise.

At the last judgement, a person's entire sum of good deeds will be weighed on the scales against the bad deeds, and if the good deeds outweigh the bad deeds, the person will be allowed to enter paradise. A Muslim who has done few good deeds and has not keep the duties and obligations of Islam has little hope of Paradise, and even if he has done numerous good deeds there is always the worry that the bad deeds might outweigh the good deeds. Salvation is by works alone.

Allah decides who will be saved and who will be damned

In the final analysis, "Allah wills what he wills". *Sura* 14:4 reads, "Now Allah leaves straying those whom He pleases and guides whom He pleases". *Sura* 7:178 supports this teaching. "Whom Allah doth guide – He is on the right path: Whom he rejects from His guidance – such are the persons who perish". Allah decides who will be saved and who will be damned.

In the light of these verses, Muslim theologians developed the concept of God's eternal decree. God has determined all things in advance and has written then down in the eternal book of his decrees. These include human actions. Thus, Allah decides a person's salvation and damnation before their birth, and their personal history is merely the working out of Allah's decree. Muslims hope the final day will reveal that the decree of the Divine has been favourable to them. Consistent with their view, however, they will not be inclined to say, "I am saved", but rather to say, "I am saved if God wills".

There is only one true God and all other ways are lost

The Ten Commandments in Exodus: (20:3) make it clear that there is one true God. This is followed through in the New Testament with passages such as 1 Corinthians 8:6: "Yet for us there is but one God, the Father, from whom all things came and for whom we live; and there is but one Lord, Jesus Christ, through whom all things came and through whom we live. And in Ephesians 4:4-6 we read: "There is one body and one Spirit-just as you were called to one hope when you were called-one Lord, one faith, one baptism; one God and father of all , who is over all and through all and in all."

A good starting point for further conversation is Mark 12:28-29, as Muslims would agree with this: "'Of all the command-ments which is the most important?' 'The most important one,' answered Jesus 'is this: "Hear, O Israel, the Lord our God, the Lord is one"'"

However, it is important in our evangelism to Muslims to point out that we believe in one God and not three gods. As well as pointing out that we believe in one God we should mention that God is a triune God of Father, God the Son and God the Holy Spirit.

It says very clearly in the Bible that there is salvation in no other but Jesus Christ and all other ways are lost. This means that anyone who does not accept Jesus as Lord and Saviour is going to a lost eternity. We have a responsibility as Christians to share the Good News of Jesus Christ to those we come across.

The end times in Islam

Islam's end-time scenario is radically different from Christianity. Muslims believe in the lesser and greater signs of the Hour. They believe that humankind will reach a state of great suffering and then the awaited Mahdi will appear. He will be the first of the greater signs of the Hour.

The Mahdi will rule until the False Messiah (*al-Masikh al Dajjal*), who will spread oppression and corruption, appears. The false Messiah will destroy humankind and the earth will witness the greatest tribulation in its history. Then *Isa* will descend to earth and bring justice. He will kill the false Messiah ushering in a period of safety and security.

Gog and Magog will then appear and surprise humankind and corruption will take over again. Then *Isa* prays and Gog and Magog will die. Later, *Isa* will die and be buried alongside Muhammad. This will be followed by the appearance of the Beast, which will lead to the Day of Judgement.

Conclusions

As Christians we see Judaism as a preparation for the coming of Christ. Islam teaches that the Jews corrupted their Scriptures, so God sent the *Injil* for the Christians. When they in turn corrupted their Scriptures, God then sent the Quran as the final revelation of God to humankind, and Muhammad as the final prophet. Muslims say that the Quran has superseded the New Testament and see Judaism and Christianity as paving the way for the coming of Islam.

The Christian idea of revelation is that God works in and through history using the prophets and apostles, who are all set in an historical framework. Muslims ignore history. For example the historical Jesus is denied by the Quran, in favour of the Quran's statements about him. For Islam the Quran's statements bears more weight than the facts set in history. All historical evidence is denied.

In Christianity we have the freedom to critique, and over the years our Scriptures have been subject to rigorous textual criticism and source analysis. Islam as a religion cannot be critiqued or criticised in this way, as the Quran is considered to be the actual words of God. Muslims consider it blasphemy to criticise the words of God. Thus different rules apply to the two religions. Islam needs to be analysed in the light of modern theological scholarship.

Islamic *dawa* or mission

Islam has a *dawa* or worldwide missionary agenda and is actively seeking converts. In the Western world hundreds of Christians are converting to Islam, principally women, many of whom are unaware of the implications of their actions. Women usually convert to Islam when they marry a Muslim man. What they do not realise is that in Islam there is no casual friendship between the sexes and as a result of even just a casual conversation with a Muslim man a woman can eventually end up in marrying him. Many Western women marry Muslim men for what they think is love but find out in a short while that all the man wanted was a visa and an economic future in the West. After the period required by immigration the man often leaves her.

But many western and Christian men are also converting out of conviction that Islam is the true path to God. The implications are far-reaching with regard to their faith. How is it they are converting? If a person is a Christian and does not know about their faith they can think that both religions are so close that it does not matter which one they follow. In Islam the religion is all set out very clearly and simply, and is basically a set of rules that covers all situations and circumstances. In comparison Christianity seems to be very complex and a private, individual faith. Islam emphasises the community, and the community spirit that exists in Islam can be very welcoming and appealing.

APPENDIX

The Gospel of Barnabas

A Christian discussing matters of faith with a Muslim may find their friend alluding to the "Gospel of Barnabas". This document is believed by many Muslims to contain the ultimate truth about the life and teaching of Jesus. Some even hold that it is the true and original *Injil*, for which Christians later substituted the New Testament.

The book professes to be a gospel written by the Apostle Barnabas. The author also claims that he, Barnabas, was one of the twelve disciples of Jesus, for which there is no support in the real Gospels. Furthermore, his denunciation of the Apostle Paul's teachings discounts the close and supportive relationship which existed between Paul and Barnabas according to the New Testament. The book denies that Jesus is the Son of God and portrays Him as a fore-runner (like John the Baptist) who proclaimed the future coming of Muhammad. It also denies the crucifixion. In addition, it even contradicts the Quran by declaring that

Muhammad will be the Messiah, whereas the Gospels and Quran agree that this title belongs to Jesus alone. Such evidence, along with geographical and historical errors, shows that the Barnabas of the New Testament is not the author of this book.

Various references in the "Gospel of Barnabas" point to its having been written in the Middle Ages, not earlier than the fourteenth century, i.e. well over a thousand years after Christ and 700 years after Muhammad. The book contains most of the stories found in the four Gospel accounts in the New Testament, but with many things artfully turned in favour of Islam. A general study of its contents and authorship shows that it is a clumsy attempt to forge a life of Jesus consonant with the profile of him in the Quran and Islamic tradition.

An English translation of the "Gospel of Barnabas" by Lonsdale and Laura Ragg was reprinted in Pakistan in the 1970s and circulated in large numbers.

For further reading see John Gilchrist's *Origins and Sources of the Gospel of Barnabas*.

The Gospel of Barnabas reprinted from Patrick Sookhdeo, *A Christian's Pocket Guide to Islam*, Pewsey: Publishing, 2005, pp. 87-88.

Glossary

Abdullah	father of Muhammad; full name: Abdallah ibn Abd al-Muttalib
Abd al-Muttalib	grand-father of Muhammad; also known as Shaybah ibn Hashim
Abu Talib	an uncle of Muhammad and father of 'Ali ibn Abi Talib, the fourth Caliph
adhan	the call to prayer
ahadith	see *"hadith"*
ahl-al-kitab	people of the book (i.e. Jews and Christians)
Ahmadis / Ahmadiyyas	an unorthodox Muslim sect from Pakistan/India, proscribed in some Muslim countries
Aisha	daughter of Abu Bakr and the favourite wife of Muhammad

'Ali ibn Abu Talib	cousin of Muhammad; eventually the fourth Caliph
Allah	the Arabic word for "God", also used by Arab Christians
amin	"Amen" in Arabic
Aramaic	a Semitic language of the Near East
Assyria	an ancient Semitic speaking Mesopotamian kingdom from the early 2nd century BC to 612 BC
Azar	Terah in the Bible; the father of Abraham
Al-Azraqi	a 9th century Islamic historian and chronicler; author of *Kitab Akhbar Makka* (*Book of Reports about Mecca*)
Babylonia	an ancient empire in the lower Euphrates valley from the early 2nd millennia to the 6th Century BC
baitu-llah	"House of Allah"; the *Kaba*
baraka	a Quranic term for blessing or favour from Allah
bismillah	in the name of Allah
burqa	Urdu term for clothing that envelops a woman in public, covering her whole body and face
Bedouin	nomadic Arabs from the Arabian Peninsula
Byzantium	the Byzantine Empire; the Greek-speaking part of the Roman Empire in the Middle Ages. Its capital was Constantinople, which in 1453 it fell

	to the Ottoman sultan Mehmed II and was renamed Istanbul
caliph	in Arabic *khalifah*; successor, vice-regent, the title used by Sunnis for the supreme spiritual and political leader of the whole Muslim community worldwide (Shias use the word *"imam"*)
Dajjal	the Antichrist
dawa/dawah	Islamic mission
dhimmi	non-Muslims in an Islamic society, subjugated people, treated as second-class
Docetics	those who practise Docetism; the gnostic doctrine that Christ's body was without any true reality and any sufferings were therefore only apparent
du'a	voluntary petitions in prayer
Elohim	The Hebrew word meaning the one and only God of Israel in the Old Testament. Used over 2,000 times in the Bible and often preceded by the definite article as *"ha-Elohim"* (The True God)
Ebionites	a Jewish Christian movement that existed during the early centuries of the Christian era
Eid-ul-fitr	see *"id-ul-fitr"*
al-fatihah	the first *sura* of the Quran

Fatima	daughter of Muhammad and his first wife Khadija
fitrah	a state of harmony and goodness between man, creation and Allah, such as existed in the Garden of Eden
Gabriel/Jibril	in Islam, the angel who gave Muhammad the revelations of the Quran
hadith (pl. *ahadith*)	tradition or report of a precedent set by Muhammad or his early followers
hajj	the annual pilgrimage to Mecca, to be performed by the believer once in a lifetime if economically possible
hajji or *hadji*	one who has made the pilgrimage to Mecca
hijab	literally "partition" or "curtain"; the institution of the seclusion of women; often used to mean the woman's head covering which conceals face, neck, hair and sometimes face
hijra	migration; Muhammad's flight from Mecca to Medina in AD 622, which was used as the starting point of the Islamic calendar
Harut and Marut	two angels mentioned in the Quran
houris	the female companions, supposedly perpetual virgins, of the saved in

	Paradise, whose main function is to provide sexual favours
Iblis	one of the names of the devil
id-ul-fitr	the feast that is observed when the fasting month of Ramadan is ended
id-ul-adha	the feast of sacrifice observed seventy days after the end of the fast of Ramadan
Ilyas	the Quranic name for the Biblical prophet Elijah
imam	leader of a mosque. (In Shia Islam "*imam*" is the term used for the leader of the whole Muslim community worldwide)
Injil	the revelation made by Allah to Jesus; the word occurs ten times in the Quran. Strictly speaking it refers to the Gospels only, but is sometimes applied to the whole New Testament
Isa	the Quranic term for Jesus; in which he is known as Isa ibn Maryam (Jesus, Son of Mary)
isha	the night prayer (the fifth prayer time of the day)
Ishaq	the Biblical prophet Isaac; son of Abraham
Ishmael/Ismail	the Biblical character Ishmael; son of Abraham

jahiliyya	the state of pagan ignorance and immorality in pre-Islamic Arabian society
jannah	literally "garden"; a term used for paradise
jihad	literally "striving". The term has a variety of interpretations including (1) spiritual struggle for moral purity (2) trying to correct wrong and support right by words and actions (3) military war in the name of Allah, against non-Muslims with the aim of spreading Islam, against apostates from Islam, or against Muslims with unorthodox theology
jinn or jinni	a spirit, created by Allah. There are some good *jinn*, but many are evil.
jizya	tax payable by *dhimmi*, as a sign of their subjugation to Muslims
Kaba	cube-shaped shrine at Mecca
karama	Marvels, or miracles. These supernatural acts using power given by Allah are performed by the "friends of Allah". In Sufi literature, especially, there abound stories of saints miracles.
Khadija	first wife of Muhammad; died in 619 AD
kitab (pl. *kutub*)	book
kitab al-Yahud	'the book of the Jews'
laylat al-qadr	see 'Night of Power'

Madrassas	a traditional school for learning Islamic studies
Mahdi	literally 'rightly guided one', whose return is awaited by Shia Muslims
Mecca	the birthplace of Muhammad and now city of pilgrimage in Saudi Arabia
Medina	the city of Muhammad's emigration according to the Quran; today in western Saudi Arabia
Midrash	a Jewish commentary on part of the Hebrew Scriptures
mihrab	niche in wall of mosque, indicating direction of prayer (towards Mecca)
Mishna	a written collection of Jewish oral traditions
Monophysite	a person who believes that there is only one inseparable nature in the person of Jesus Christ
Mount Hira	the mountain where, according to Islamic tradition, Muhammad would retreat to meditate in a cave at the summit
muezzin	the one who gives out the call to prayer from the mosque
mufti	Sunni scholar, who is an interpreter and expounder of sharia; one who is authorised to issue fatwas
mullah	a religious teacher. The term is more common in Pakistan and India

Najran	a city and region in southern Arabia near Yemen, before Islam, it was an oasis with a Christian population and the seat of a bishopric
Nestorians	Christians who hold to the teachings of the theologian Nestorius (386-450). They emphasise a distinction between the human and divine natures of Jesus Christ
Night of Power	As referred to in *sura* 97; it occurs during the month of Ramadan each year. According to Muslim tradition, it is the night that marked the beginning of the revelation of the Quran to Muhammad and his mission of delivering it to humankind.
pir	Persian term for a Sufi holy man, "saint" or spiritual guide; may also be known as a *murshid* or a sheikh
Qabil and Habil	the Quranic terms for the Biblical characters Cain and Abel from the book of Genesis
qibla	direction to which one faces while praying i.e. towards Mecca
Quran	the Muslims' holy book
Quraysh	the tribe of Mecca
Ar-Rajim	literally meaning "the stoned"; it is a description in the Quran to the Devil
Ramadan	the ninth month in the Islamic calendar, the fasting month

Ruh al-Qudus	The Arabic term for the Holy Spirit; according to the Quran: to assist *Isa* (Jesus) and to bring Muhammad the Quranic revelation. The phrase occurs four times in the Quran. Some Muslim commentators have identified it with Gabriel and others with the created spirit from Allah.
Sabians/Sabeans	a people group named in the Quran, as having a religion revealed by Allah
sadaqa	voluntary offerings made at *id-ul-fitr*
salat	Muslim ritual prayer recited five times a day
Sassanids	a major pre-Islamic dynasty that ruled Persia and Mesopotamia from the third century until it was overthrown by Muslim forces in 651
sawm	the act of fasting
shahada	Islamic creed
shahid	the Arabic term for "witness"; in Islam it means a "martyr" (one who dies while striving for the cause of Islam)
Sharia	Islamic religious law. *Shariat* is the Urdu word
Shaytan	one of the names of the devil
sheikh / shaykh	literally "old man" or elder. This title can be given to heads of religious orders, Quranic scholars, jurists, those who preach and lead

	prayers in the mosque, and to Sufi saints. It is also used for a village elder or tribal chief.
Shema	the Jewish creed: "Hear, O Israel: the Lord our God, the Lord is one" (Deuteronomy 6:4)
Shia/Shi'ah	the Muslim sect that believes that the rightful successor to Muhammad was Ali, his closest relative
shirk	associating anyone with Allah as a co-deity. The worst sin in Islam
Sufi	a mystic
sunna	literally "a trodden path"; the customs of Muhammad and his early followers who knew him personally
Sunni	literally "one of the path"; orthodox Islam; the majority, who follow the successors of Muhammad by election
sura	literally "a row or series"; used exclusively for chapters of the Quran
Ta'ala	a pre-Islamic tribal god
Targum	spoken Jewish paraphrases, explanations and expansions of the Hebrew Scriptures
tawhid	unity, oneness; basic doctrine of Islam declaring the absolute oneness of Allah
tayammum	purification by sand or earth (when water is not procurable)

Tefilah	Hebrew for prayer, within Judaism; with a strong emphasis on blessings and benedictions.
Torah/Tawrat	the law of Moses, the first five books of the Old Testament, 'taurat' in Urdu
wudu/wadu	lesser ablution, as distinguished from *ghusl*
Yathrib	see "Medina"
Yunus	the Quranic name for the Biblical prophet Jonah
Zabur	Psalms
zakat	the alms due from every Muslim
Zamzam	a well that is located in Mecca, Saudi Arabia; near the *Kaba*, which according to Islam appeared to Hagar and Ishmael in the desert
Zoroastrians	followers of the religion of Zoroastrianism, founded by Zoroaster in the 1st millennium BC and was practised by the majority in Persia and parts of Central Asia before the conquest of these areas by Muslim forces. They a people group named in the Quran as having a religion revealed by Allah

Glossary reprinted from Patrick Sookhdeo, *A Pocket Guide to Islam*, Pewsey: Isaac Publishing, 2010, pp. 113-123.

Table Comparing The Differences Between Islam And Christianity

As Islam increasingly confronts us in our modern world it becomes necessary to understand the differences between Islam and Christianity. This concise table of the main traditional beliefs in each religion is designed to make our understanding easy. For many people both religions appear similar, but are they really? Do they share the same prophets? Does each teach the same about Jesus? This helpful table addresses these and other important differences.

ISLAM	CHRISTIANITY
THE QURAN	**THE BIBLE**
It has 114 chapters (*suras*) and is roughly the size of the New Testament. The *suras* are put together in order of length, the longest ones at the beginning and the shortest at the end, except the first *sura* The Opening (*al-Fatihah*). Muslims believe the Quran is uncreated, eternally preserved on a tablet in heaven, known as the "Mother of the Book" (*sura* 85:21-22). That is was communicated word-for-word to Muhammad in Arabic over a period of 23 years (*sura* 12:1-2). Muslims believe the angel Gabriel, sent by Allah, visited Muhammad with the revelations (*sura* 26:193).	It consists of 66 books written over a period of 1400 years by over 40 authors in Hebrew, Aramaic and Greek.
	They wrote under the inspiration of the Holy Spirit: *"...no prophecy of Scripture came about by the prophet's own interpretation. For prophecy never had its origin in the human will, but prophets, though human, spoke from God as they were carried along by the Holy Spirit"* (2 Peter 1:20-21).
It is considered by Muslims to be the ultimate error-free authority on Islam.	**The Bible is the infallible word of God and is the ultimate authority for Christians.**
The Quran is considered the final revelation of Allah to mankind, after the Torah (*Taurat*) of Moses, the Psalms (*Zabur*) of David and the Gospel (*Injil*) of Jesus. Muslims say that these Scriptures (except the Quran) have been corrupted over time by the Jews and Christians.	

ISLAM	CHRISTIANITY
THE QURAN (cont.)	
Muslims believe that the Bible and all other holy books have been superseded by the Quran.	
Many of the versus (*suras*) in the Quran are contradictory. Some of these are overcome by the Doctrine of Abrogation. This means that many of the *suras* that were revealed earlier in Muhammad's life are superseded by those that were revealed at a later date (*suras* 2:106, 13:39).	
ALLAH (GOD)	**GOD**
God is known as Allah. He is absolute oneness (*tawheed*). *sura* 112 states 'He is Allah, the One and Only.	God is one in an eternal Trinity, made up of the Father, Son and Holy Spirit. Not three gods, rather a unity of the Godhead: *"In the beginning God…"*, *"Therefore go and make disciples of all nations, baptising them in the name of the Father and of the Son and of the Holy Spirit"* (Genesis 1:1, Matthew 28:19).
To put anyone or anything equal to Allah is the sin of *shirk* (polytheism). Therefore he has no equal partner, children or son and therefore there is no Trinity (*tathlith*) (*sura* 4:171).	
Muslims are confused about the Christian Trinity as they believe it is God the father, Mary the mother and Jesus the son (*sura* 5:116).	

ISLAM	CHRISTIANITY
ALLAH IS NOT A GOD OF LOVE Allah is not a god of love. He does not love sinners (*suras* 2:276, 3:57, 4:107).	**GOD IS LOVE** It was out of His love for mankind that God sent His son: *"For God so loved the world that He gave His one and only Son, that whoever believes in Him shall not perish but have eternal life." "But God demonstrates his own love for us in this: While we were still sinners Christ died for us"* (John 3:16, Roman 5:8).
ALLAH IS NOT FATHER Allah is unknowable and is not referred to as "father". He is transcendent (*tanzih*) and powerful.	**GOD IS FATHER** God has adopted those who believe on His Son as his heavenly children: *"Dear friends, now we are children of God"* (1 John 3:2). God is a knowable, heavenly father. He is transcendent and imminent; full of grace and glory: *"'Am I only a God nearby" declares the Lord, 'and not a God far away? Who can hide in secret places so that I cannot see them?' declares the Lord. 'Do not I fill heaven and earth?' declares the Lord"* (Jeremiah 23:23-24).

ISLAM	CHRISTIANITY
ALLAH IS CREATOR Allah is the creator of the world (*suras* 23:14, 6:102, 13:16).	**GOD IS CREATOR** God is almighty, the Creator and sustainer of the world (Genesis 1:1, 148:5).
ALLAH HAS NOT REVEALED HIMSELF TO MANKIND Allah is self-sufficient (*sura* 31:26). Allah predetermines everything; the destiny of creation is fixed (*suras* 25:2, 65:3). He determines all according to his mercy and wisdom (*suras* 2:216, 42:27). All things are decreed by Allah (*sura* 85:16). He can decree both good and evil.	**GOD HAS REVEALED HIMSELF IN JESUS** He has revealed Himself to mankind in the person of Jesus: "Jesus answered: *'…Anyone who has seen me has seen the Father'*" (John 14:9).
ATTRIBUTES AND ACTIONS Allah is best understood from his traditional 99 most beautiful names (*sura* 7:180) although there are more than 99 found in the Quran. For example, they reveal his attributes: holy, eternal, the one, the hidden, the manifest, the light, the most high, the omniscient, the living, the omnipotent, the seeing, the hearing, the wise, the dominator, the strong and the	**ATTRIBUTES AND ACTIONS** God is described in the Bible as eternal, glorious, almighty, merciful, holy, righteous, forgiving, omnipotent, incomparable and omniscient. And his actions are loving, just and wise.

ISLAM	CHRISTIANITY
ATTRIBUTES AND ACTIONS (cont.) crafty one (*suras* 3:54, 8:30). And they reveal his actions: the guide, the provider, the gentle, the just, the merciful, the harmer, the withholder, the avenger, the abaser and the one who leads astray (*sura* 6:39). **Some of Allah's actions and attributes are not consistent with the Biblical God.**	
JESUS *(Isa)* In the Quran, Jesus' name is "*Isa*", and is often called "Isa son of Mary". In most places he is called "apostle of Allah"(*sura* 3:49), but also "servant of Allah" (*sura* 19:30), "al-Masih"(the "Messiah", but not in the specific Biblical meaning) (*sura* 3:45), "a sign for mankind" (*sura* 19:21), a "word of Allah" (*sura* 4:171) and "a spirit from him"(*sura* 21:91).	**JESUS** The Bible has many names for Jesus, some are: Creator, Saviour, the Word, Holy One, Image of the invisible God, Lord, Prince of Peace, Mediator and Messiah.
VIRGIN BIRTH *Isa*/Jesus was born of the virgin Mary, and was fully human (*sura* 3:42-47).	**VIRGIN BIRTH** Jesus was born of the virgin Mary and was fully human: *"the Word became flesh and made His dwelling among us"* (John 1:14).

ISLAM	CHRISTIANITY
JESUS IS NOT THE SON OF GOD Jesus is a created being and is only a man (*suras* 3:59, 5:75). Jesus is not the son of God or divine (*suras* 9:30, 19:34-35).	**JESUS IS THE SON OF GOD** Jesus is fully human and fully divine. He is the Son of God: *"And a voice from heaven said, 'This is my Son, whom I love; with Him I am well pleased'"* (Matthew 3:17, John 1:14, 18).
JESUS IS A PROPHET Jesus is a great prophet sent by Allah who is held in honour in this world and in the hereafter (*sura* 3:45). He announces Muhammad as the next and last prophet (*sura* 61:6)	**JESUS IS THE FULFIL-MENT OF THE PROPHETS** Jesus is the fulfilment of the law and the prophets: *"Do not think that I [Jesus] have come to abolish the Law of the Prophets; I have not come to abolish them but to fulfil them"* (Matthew 5:17).
JESUS PERFORMED MIRACLES Jesus was a miracle-worker. "With the permission of God" he made a clay bird come to life (the Arabic word *khalaqa* is used only for God's creating work). He healed, raised the dead and knew the unknown (*sura* 3:49).	**JESUS PERFORMED MIRACLES** Jesus performed miracles during His earthly ministry to reveal His glory: *"This, the first of His miraculous signs, Jesus performed at Cana in Galilee. He thus revealed His glory, and His disciples put their faith in Him"*. (John 2:11). This included bringing the dead to life: *"...Jesus called in a loud voice, 'Lazarus come out!' The dead man came out, his hands and feet wrapped with strips of linen, and a cloth around his face"* (John 11:43-44).

ISLAM	CHRISTIANITY
JESUS DID NOT DIE ON THE CROSS OR RISE FROM THE DEAD Jesus did not die on a cross and he did not rise from the dead. Another man died in the place of Jesus on the cross. Muslims believe that Allah would not allow one of his prophets to die a death of disgrace (*sura* 4:157).	**JESUS DIED ON THE CROSS AND ROSE AGAIN** Jesus died on a cross because of the sin of mankind. *"It was the third hour when they crucified Him"*. (Mark 15:25). He defeated death and was raised from the dead on the third day: *"When Jesus rose early on the first day of the week, he appeared to Mary Magdalene…"* (1 Corinthians 15:3-8, Romans 4:25).
JESUS ASCENDED INTO HEAVEN Muslims believe that Jesus ascended to heaven, where he still lives and will one day return (*suras* 3:55, 4:157-8).	**JESUS ASCENDED INTO HEAVEN** He ascended into heaven and now sits at the right hand of God the Father until the second-coming: *"After the Lord Jesus had spoken to them, He was taken up into heaven and He sat at the right hand of God"* (Mark 16:19).
JESUS WILL COME AGAIN BUT AS A MUSLIM Jesus will return to earth as a Muslim at the second-coming, he will get married, have children, convert all Christians to Islam, some traditions say destroy the Jews, break all crosses, rule as king	**JESUS WILL COME AGAIN AS KING OF KINGS AND LORD OF LORDS** *"They will see the Son of Man coming on the clouds of the sky, with power and great glory. And he will send his angels with a loud trumpet call, and they will gather his*

ISLAM	CHRISTIANITY
JESUS WILL COME AGAIN BUT AS A MUSLIM (cont.)	**JESUS WILL COME AGAIN AS KING OF KINGS AND LORD OF LORDS (cont.)**
of the Muslims, kill all swine, die and be buried alongside Muhammad in Medina (*Sahih Muslim* vol 1, bk 1, c 71, p.104).	*elect from the four winds, from one end of the heavens to the other"* (Matthew 24:30-31).
HOLY SPIRIT The Quran speaks only very vaguely about a spirit, some-times called "holy spirit" (*rul al-qudus*) (*sura* 16:102). Muslims identify him with angel Gabriel.	**HOLY SPIRIT** The Holy Spirit is part of the triune Godhead: *"Again Jesus said, 'Peace be upon you! As the Father has sent me, I am sending you'. And with that he breathed on them and said, 'Receive the Holy Spirit'"* (John 20:21-22).
CREATION Allah created the heavens and the earth in six days (*suras* 29:44, 50:38).	**CREATION** God created the universe in six days. *"In the beginning God created the heavens and the earth"* (Genesis 1:1).
CREATION OF MANKIND Allah created man from either clay or a blood-clot to wor-ship and obey him (*suras* 32:7, 96:2, 51:56).	**CREATION OF MANKIND** God created man in his own image: *"So God created human beings in his own image, in the image of God he created them; male and female he created them"* (Genesis 1:27).

ISLAM	CHRISTIANITY
ADAM AND EVE CREATED WEAK Adam was created "weak", i.e. not perfect (*sura* 4:28).	**ADAM AND EVE CREATED SINLESS** God created Adam and Eve innocent and sinless.
THE FALL OF MAN The story of mankind's fall was actually an equal challenge between Allah and Satan (*suras* 7:11-17, 24). Satan was disobedient to God because he did not prostrate before Adam. Adam and Eve got caught up in this challenge and were tempted by Satan in Paradise (Heaven).	**THE FALL OF MAN** Satan tempted Eve to sin. Eve then tempted Adam. They both disobeyed God and ate of the forbidden fruit: *"When the women saw that the fruit of the tree was good for food…she took some and ate it. She also gave some to her husband, who was with her, and he ate it"* (Genesis 3:6). In Christianity Adam and Eve were tempted on earth.
THE RESULT OF THE FALL Adam and Eve repented and God accepted (*suras* 2:37, 7:23). Adam and Eve were then cast down to earth without sin (*sura* 2:36). Because their sin was a personal lapse it did not bring innate sin on the whole of mankind. **Therefore there is no need for a Saviour to pay the ransom for sin.**	**THE RESULT OF THE FALL** This sin against God resulted in their expulsion from the earthly Garden of Eden and separation from God: *"So the Lord God banished him* [Adam] *from the Garden of Eden…"* (Genesis 3:23). Their actions had the consequence of bringing sin into the world, which brought death. Man is a sinner and completely lost (Romans 6:23).

ISLAM	CHRISTIANITY
	THE RESULT OF THE FALL (cont.) **Therefore to save mankind, there needed to be a second Adam (Jesus) who would be a blood sacrifice, breaking the power of sin and healing the divide between God and mankind.**
AFTER DEATH At death the angel Izra'il separates the soul from the body (*sura* 32:11). In the grave there is an examination by the angels Munkar and Nakir, which sometimes involves torture. Prayer for the dead is beneficial (*sura* 59:10). Between death and the Judgement Day (*yaum al-hisab*) the soul rests in purgatory (*barzakh*).	**AFTER DEATH** Christ will come again to judge the world. Only God the Father knows this appointed time. Christ will come as the King-of-Kings in power and splendour, heralded in by angels. The dead will be resurrected: *"At that time people will see the Son of Man coming in clouds with great power and glory. And He will send His angels and gather His elect from the four winds, from the ends of the earth to the ends of the heavens"* (Mark 13:26-27).
JUDGEMENT DAY (yaum ad-din) The angel Israf'il will blow the trumpet (*sur*) to announce the last day. The dead will be resurrected (*sura* 39:67-75). The balance of the good and bad	**JUDGEMENT DAY** All must appear before the judgement seat of Christ. Those who did not put their faith in Christ will be judged with eternal punishment. For the Christian, it is only their

ISLAM	CHRISTIANITY
JUDGEMENT DAY (yaum ad-din) (cont.)	**JUDGEMENT DAY (cont.)**
deeds will be weighed. (*suras* 21:47, 23:102-3). There will be a sharp bridge for all humanity to cross (the bridge of *sirat*) over hell fire. Those whose good deeds exceed their bad deeds will pass over it. **Heaven in Islam is through works, but there is no assurance and nothing can be guaranteed.**	works that will be judged: *"For we must all appear before the judgement seat of Christ, that everyone may receive what is due them for the things done while in the body, whether good or bad"* (2 Corinthians 5:10, John 3:18, Matthew 25:31-46).
SIGNS OF THE END TIMES	**SIGNS OF THE END TIMES**
Only Allah and Jesus know when the Judgement Day will be. Jesus has knowledge of the hour (*sura* 43:61). The signs of the last days are the lesser signs which are: an increase of injustice, sin, faithlessness, shamelessness and tribulation. The greater signs will be the Antichrist (*Dajjal*), the Beast of the earth, the rising of the sun in the West, the return of Jesus, Gog and Magog and also the appearance of the Mahdi. On Judgement Day all creatures will die and the universe will be destroyed. **There are many signs of the end times that are similar in both religions.**	The signs of the end times include: wars, natural disasters, false prophets and an increase of sin in the world: *"...many will come in my [Jesus] name, claiming 'I am the Christ', and will deceive many. You will hear of wars and rumours of wars, but see to it that you are not alarmed. Such things must happen, but the end is still to come. Nation will rise against nation...There will be famines and earthquakes..."'* (Matthew 24:4-8). The earth will be burnt up with fire. There will be a new heaven and a new earth for the believers to dwell in: *"...for the first heaven and the first earth had passed away..."* (Revelation 21:1).

ISLAM	CHRISTIANITY
SIN Sin is disobedience to divine law. It is only accountable if done intentionally. There are major and minor sins.	**SIN** Sin is any failure to conform to the moral law of God in act, attitude or nature.
HUMANS ARE NOT SINFUL God found Muhammad when he was astray (pre-inspiration *sura* 93:7), Muhammad asked for forgiveness (*sura* 47:19), God guided him and granted him forgiveness (*sura* 48:2). Children are born sinless. Man is not innately sinful and has the choice whether to sin or not.	**HUMANS ARE SINFUL BY THEIR NATURE** Man is innately sinful because he inherited the nature that came from the fallen first man (Adam). *"Therefore, just as sin entered the world through one man, and death through sin, and in this way death came to all people, because all sinned..."* (Romans 5:12).
JESUS WAS FAULTLESS He said: "I am only a messenger of thy Lord, that I may bestow on thee a faultless son" *(sura 19:19).*	**JESUS WAS SINLESS** Jesus was without sin, but God made him share our nature and on the cross became sin that we might share the righteousness of God: *"God made Him who had no sin to be sin for us, so that in Him we might become the righteousness of God"* (2 Corinthians 5:21).

ISLAM	CHRISTIANITY
NO CONCEPT OF SALVATION	**SALVATION THROUGH FAITH**
Mankind must submit to Allah to find forgiveness. There is no atonement in Islam (*sura* 17:15). There is no concept of salvation because Allah "forgives whom he pleases, and punishes whom he pleases" (*sura* 2:284). Only works are taken into account. The *hadiths* serve as a blue-print of how a Muslim should live his life. The Quran and *hadith* give five obligatory duties for Muslims to perform. These five pillars are: the confession of faith, prayer, fasting, almsgiving and pil-grimage to Mecca.	Salvation is by faith in the saving action of Jesus on the cross and not by works. God's grace is a free gift; people do not have to work to gain this gift of salvation: *"For it is by grace you have been saved, through faith – and this not from yourselves, it is the gift of God – not by works, so that no-one can boast"* (Ephesians 2:8-9). Good works are the fruit of this salvation.
Heaven for a Muslim is by guidance (*huda*) and good works. There is no certainty.	By believing that Jesus died and rose again brings recon-ciliation with God, forgiveness of one's sins and assurance of salvation: *"...Their* [human] *sins and lawless acts I* [God] *will remember no more"* (Hebrews 10:17). **Salvation Through Faith (cont.)**
	In Christianity we have the certainty of salvation through Christ's atone-ment, not by good works.
HEAVEN (Paradise)	**HEAVEN**
Paradise (*janna, firdous*) is a sensuous place of pleasure and joy. Allah will not be in fellowship with the righteous in paradise. The righteous will	Heaven is a perfect place of eternal joy, worship and holi-ness, where God will be wor-shipped and served forever: *"the twenty-four elders fall*

ISLAM	CHRISTIANITY
HEAVEN (Paradise) (cont.)	**HEAVEN (cont.)**
find there beautiful women (*houris*), full goblets of drink, rich carpets and couches (*suras* 56:11-38, 88:8-16). There will be a plentiful supply of food, fountains of drink and rivers of milk, wine and honey (*suras* 47:15, 56:8-38). **In Islam heaven is a place of sensual delights and is not centred on Allah.** Martyrs will have their sins blotted out by Allah and will enter into paradise immediately (*sura* 3:169). There is no guarantee of direct entry into paradise for any other Muslim. **Women can only get to heaven by being completely obedient to their husbands.** *Sahih Al Bukhari, 161:2*	*down before Him who sits on the throne, and worship Him who lives for ever and ever..."* (Revelation 4:10-11, 5:13). In heaven there will be no pain, death or marriage: *"When the dead rise, they will neither marry nor be given in marriage"* (Mark 12:25). Only those who have put their faith in Christ can enter heaven. They will be rewarded by God for their faithfulness.
HELL	**HELL**
Hell (*al-Nar or Jahannum*) is a place of fiery torment for sinners (Sura 78:21-30). Those in hell will 'neither die nor live' (*sura* 87:13). There will be boiling water to drink and bitter food to eat (*sura* 88:5-7). Hell will have 7 chambers. The first is purgatorial fire (*Jahannum*) for Muslims. The second is flam-	The Bible presents hell as a place of eternal suffering and punishment: *"Then they [those who do not know Christ] will go away to eternal punishment, but the righteous to eternal life"*, *"...it is better for you to enter the kingdom of God with one eye than to have two eyes and be thrown*

ISLAM	CHRISTIANITY
HELL (cont.)	**HELL (cont.)**
ing fire (*Laza*) for Christians, which is not eternal. The third is the raging fire (*Hutama*) for Jews, which is not eternal (*sura* 104:4). The fourth is the blazing fire (*Sa'ir*) for Sabians, which is not eternal (*sura* 2:62). The fifth is the scorching fire (*Sakar*) for Zoroastrians. The sixth is the fierce fire (*Jahim*), for idolaters and polytheists which is eternal. The seventh is the abyss (*Hawiya*) for hypocrites (*sura* 101:9). Muhammad intercedes for Muslims in purgatory (*sura* 5:69).	*in to hell, where...the fire is not quenched"* (Matthew 25:46, Mark 9:47-48). Those who do not repent of their sin and believe in Christ will end up in hell: *"Jesus said to her [Martha], "I am the resurrection and the life. Those who believe in me will live, even though they die; and whoever lives and believes in me will never die. Do you believe this?"'* (John 11:25).
In the *hadith* it is recorded that Muhammad reported that hell would be full of poor people and women (*Sahih Al Bukhari* 301:1).	**Through faith in Christ all Christians (men and women equally) have the certainty of heaven.**
PROPHETS	**PROPHETS**
These are the people whom Allah chose and prepared to remind mankind of himself and to make known his commands. They are truthful, miracle-workers, sinless and infallible. Each had the same message and they were often treated badly by unbelievers (*sura* 21: 25, 36). Adam was the first prophet. Some more prominent prophets are:	The prophets of the Old and New Testament are chosen by God, not because of their sinless life but because of their obedience to God. With all the prophets of the Old and New Testament Jesus is considered greater. *"In the past God spoke to our ancestors through the prophets at many times and in various*

ISLAM	CHRISTIANITY
PROPHETS (cont.)	**PROPHETS (cont.)**
Noah, the preacher of Allah; Abraham, the friend of Allah; Moses, the speaker with Allah; John the Baptist and Isa (Jesus). There are three pre-Islamic prophets Hud, prophet to the ancient tribe of Ad, Salih, prophet to the tribe of Thamud and Shu'aib prophet to the tribe of Madyan. Muslims believe that Muhammad is the last and seal of the prophets. He is the greatest of the prophets (*suras* 33:40, 61:6).	*ways, but in these last days He has spoken to us by His Son, whom He appointed heir of all things, and through whom He made the universe"* (Hebrews 1:1-2). Jesus had apostles to help Him during His earthly ministry. They then took His Gospel to the world.
THE SONS OF IBRAHIM ISHMAEL & ISAAC	**THE SONS OF ABRAHAM ISHMAEL & ISAAC**
Hagar (*Hajar*), Abraham's (*Ibrahim's*) maid, gave birth to Ishmael. Sarah, his wife, gave birth to Isaac (*sura* 14:39). Tradition makes Ishmael the father of the Arab people as it was through his blood-line that Muhammad would be born. Muslims believe that Abraham and Ishmael built the cube-shaped *Kaba* (house of Allah) in Mecca. (*sura* 2:124-5).	Hagar Abraham's maid gave birth to Ishmael and Sarah his wife gave birth to Isaac. *"Hagar [Abraham's maid] bore Abram a son, and Abram [later named Abraham] gave the name Ishmael to the son she had borne"* (Genesis 16:15). *"Sarah [Abraham's wife] became pregnant and bore a son to Abraham in his old age, at the very time God had promised him. Abraham gave the name Isaac to the son Sarah bore him"* (Genesis 21:2-3).

ISLAM	CHRISTIANITY
ISHMAEL: THE SON OF THE SACRIFICE	**ISAAC: THE SON OF PROMISE**
Muslims believe that Isaac was the son of promise but not the one to be sacrificed (*suras* 11:69-73, 37:112-113). Abraham's faith was tested by the order to sacrifice his son. Allah sent an angel with a ram that was sacrificed in the son's place (*sura* 37:100-111). The Quran does not mention the name of the son, tradition mentions both sons, and from the middle ages they say it was Ishmael. Ishmael is regarded as a prophet (*sura* 2:136). Abraham left Hagar and Ishmael in Mecca and Allah provided water for them to drink at a place called Zamzam. This place is visited today by Muslims on pilgrimage to Mecca.	Isaac was the chosen son, from whose blood-line the Messiah would be born: *'Then God said, "Yes, but your* [Abraham's] *wife Sarah will bear you a son, and you will call him Isaac. I will establish my covenant with him as an everlasting covenant for his descendants after him"* (Genesis 17:19). As a test of faith, *"God said* [to Abraham], *'take your son, your only son, Isaac, whom you love, and go to the region of Moriah. Sacrifice him there as a burnt offering on one of the mountains I will tell you about'"* (Genesis 22:2). At the last minute, God sent an angel to stop Abraham killing Isaac, by presenting him with a ram. Abraham withstood the test of his faith. **In the Bible it says that Abraham prepared to sacrifice his son Isaac, the son of promise, not Ishmael.**
ANGELS	**ANGELS**
Angels were created from light by Allah (*sura* 7:12). Their role is to protect believers, to praise Allah and to guard the Quran.	Angels were created by God: *"For by him all things were created: things in heaven and on earth, visible and invisible"* (Colossians 1:16). They are

ISLAM	CHRISTIANITY
ANGELS (cont.)	**ANGELS (cont.)**
The number of angels is not known, however four angels stand out: Jibr'il (Gabriel), Israf'il who blows his trumpet on Judgement Day, Mika'il (Michael) who brings the rain and Izra'il, the angel of death. There are two angels that daily record the good deeds and the bad deeds of all humans (*sura* 82:10-12).	called ministering spirits and God has commanded them to help men. *"Are not all angels ministering spirits sent to serve those who inherit salvation"* (Hebrews 1:14). They protect and deliver and guide our ways. They surround the throne of God, praise and serve him (Isaiah 6:1-6). Millions of angels are at God's command. Michael is the archangel, Gabriel is one of the most prominent angels, and is God's messenger of mercy and promise. He always bears good news. *"The angel answered, 'I am Gabriel, I stand in the presence of God, and I have been sent to speak to you and to tell you this good news'"* (Luke 1:19).
SATAN	**SATAN**
Satan was created by Allah and was originally a jinn. He lived amongst the angels in heaven and worshipped Allah. But he disobeyed Allah when he would not bow down to Adam and as a result was thrown out of heaven. (*sura* 2:34).	Satan was created by God and lived in heaven. He was the anointed cherubim and named Lucifer which means Day Star. Before the creation of the earth Satan led a heavenly rebellion against God, and was cast out of heaven forever (Isaiah 14:12-15). After Judgement Day he and

ISLAM	CHRISTIANITY
	SATAN (cont.) his fallen angels or demons will spend eternity in hell: *'Then He* [Jesus] *will say to those on His left, "depart from me, you who are cursed, into the eternal fire prepared for the devil and his angel" "And the devil who deceived them, was thrown into the lake of burning sulphur..."* (Matthew 25:41, Revelation 20:10).
JINNS Jinn are beings between angels and men that Allah created from smokeless fire and belong to the spirit world (*sura* 55:15). They were created to worship Allah (Sura 51:56). The jinn can beget children, possess humans, have an abode (e.g. trees) and can change form into cows, sheep, etc. Although theoretically neutral most jinn are considered bad. Jinn can be believers or non-believers (*suras* (6:130, 72:1-17). Satans (shaitans) are truth-concealing jinn, and Iblis (the Devil) is one (*sura* 15:50). He is a jinn who leads evil jinn. Iblis is destined to be thrown into hell fire on Judgement Day.	

ISLAM	CHRISTIANITY
FAITH	**FAITH**
Faith is the confession with the tongue that "there is no god but Allah, and Muhammad is his messenger", the internal conviction and the performing of the duties and obligations of the religion.	Faith is confessing that Jesus Christ is Lord and acknowledging that He died on the cross and rose from the dead. It is through this there is forgiveness of sins and eternal life. Faith is a personal and living relationship with God.

Table reprinted from Rosemary Sookhdeo, *Why Christian Women Convert to Islam*, 2nd US ed. McLean: Isaac Publishing, 2016, pp. 105-125.

Bibliography

Ali, 'Abdullah Yusuf *The Meaning of the Holy Qur'an*. Beltsville, Maryland: Amana Publications, 1999.

Ali, M. *Translation and Commentary on the Holy Qur'an*, 4th edition. Lahore, 1951.

Alim. Silver Spring: Maryland: ISL Software Corp., 1986-1999. Now online at http://www.alim.org/.

Ashour, Mustafa *The Jinn in the Qu'ran and the Sunna*, 3rd edition. London: Dar Al Taqwa Ltd, 1993.

Azzi, Joseph *The Priest & the Prophet: the Christian Priest, Waraqa ibn Nawfal's profound Influence upon Muhammad*. Los Angeles: The Pen Publishers, 2005.

Baljon, J. M. S. *Modern Muslim Koran Interpretation (1880-1960)*. Leiden: Brill, 1961, pp. 38-39.

Bashier, Zakaria *The Makkan Crucible*. Leicester: The Islamic Foundation, 1991.

Bell, Richard *The Origin of Islam and its Christian Environment*. London: Frank Cass and Co Ltd, 1968.

Bell, Richard *The Qur'an: Volume I*. Edinburgh: T & T Clark, 1937.

Benthall, Jonathan *Islamic Charities and Islamic Humanism in Troubled Times*. Manchester: MUP, 2016.

Bukay, David *From Muhammad to Bin Laden*. New Brunswick: Transaction Publishers, 2008.

Cragg, K. *The Event of the Qur'an*. London: George Allen & Unwin Ltd, 1971.

Crone, Patricia *Hagarism*. Cambridge: CUP, 1977.

David, Ariel 'Before Islam: When Saudi Arabia was a Jewish Kingdom', *Haaretz*, 29 November, 2017, https://www.haaretz.com/archaeology/.premium-before-islam-when-saudi-arabia-was-a-jewish-kingdom-1.5626227.

Donner, Fred M. *Muhammad and the Believers at the Origins of Islam*. Cambridge, Mass.: Harvard University Press, 2010.

Douglas, J. D. and Tenney, M. C. *Zondervan Illustrated Bible Dictionary*. Grand Rapids: Zondervan, 2011.

Emerick, Yahiya *The Complete Idiot's Guide to Understanding Islam*. Indianapolis: Alpha, 2003).

Encyclopaedia of Islam, 2nd ed., (Leiden: Brill, 1954-2004).

Geiger, Abraham *Judaism and Islam*. 1898, repr. New York: KTAV, 1970.

Gilchrist, John *Origins and Sources of the Gospel of Barnabas.* Sheffield, FFM Publications, 1979.

Gilchrist, John *Muhammad and the Religion of Islam.* Benoni, 1986.

Gilchrist, John *Muhammad: The Prophet of Islam.* Mondeor: MERCSA, 1994.

Glubb, John Bagot *The Life and Times of Muhammad.* London: The History Book Club, 1970.

Guillaume, A. *Islam.* London: Penguin, 1954, 1990.

Guillaume, A. *The Life of Muhammad: A Translation of Ibn Ishaq's Sirat Rasul Allah.* Karachi: OUP, 1998.

Kuenen, A. *The Hibbert Lectures 1882: National Religions and Universal Religions: Lectures.* London: Williams and Norgate, 1882.

Margoliouth, D. S. *Mohammed and the Rise of Islam.* New York: G P Putnam's Sons, 1906, repr. 1927.

Mohamed, Yasien *Human Nature in Islam.* Kuala Lumpur: A. S. Noordeen, 1998.

Muir, William *Life of Mahomet: Volume III.* 1861, repr. Osnabruck: Biblio Verlag, 1988.

Muir, William *The Life of Mahomet from Original Sources.* London: Smith, Elder & Co, 1877.

Neuwirth, A. et al., *The Qur'ān in Context: Historical and Literary Investigations into the Qur'ānic Milieu.* Leiden: Brill, 2010.

Newby, Gorden D. *A Concise Encyclopedia of Islam.* Oxford: Oneworld, 2002.

O'Leary, De Lacy *Arabia before Muhammad*. London: Routledge, 1927, repr. 2000.

Osman, Ghada 'Pre-Islamic Arab Converts to Christianity in Mecca and Medina; An Investigation into the Arabic Sources', *The Muslim World*, Volume 95, No 1, January 2005, https://onlinelibrary.wiley.com/doi/abs/10.1111/j.1478-1913.2005.00079.x.

Parrinder, Geoffrey *Jesus in the Qur'an*. London: Sheldon Press, 1965.

Peters, Francis E *Muhammad and the Origins of Islam*. New York: New York State University Press, 1994.

Pickthall, Marmaduke (trans.) *The Meaning of the Glorious Koran*. London: Everyman Publishers Plc, 1992.

Qutb, Sayyid *In the Shade of the Qur'an: Volume XVIII: Surahs 78-114*. Leicester: The Islamic Foundation, 2004.

Reynolds, Gabriel Said 'The Muslim Jesus: Dead or Alive?', *Bulletin of the SOAS*, Volume 72, No 2, 2009, pp. 237-258.

Roggema, Barbara 'A Christian Reading of the Qur'an: The Legend of Sergius-Bahira and its use of Qur'an and Sira' in David Thomas, ed., *Syrian Christians under Islam: The First Thousand Years*. Leiden: Brill, 2001, pp. 57-73.

Saeed, A. *Interpreting the Quran: Towards a Contemporary Approach*. London: Routledge, 2005.

Schirrmacher, Thomas *The Bible and the Koran*. Eugene, OR: Wipf & Stock, 2018.

Sookhdeo, Patrick *A Christian's Pocket Guide to Islam*, Pewsey: Isaac Publishing, 2005.

Sookhdeo, Patrick *A Pocket Guide to Islam*, Christian Pewsey: Isaac Publishing, 2010.

Sookhdeo, Rosemary *Why Christian Women Convert to Islam*, 2nd US ed. McLean: Isaac Publishing, 2016.

St Clair-Tisdall, W. *The Original Sources of the Qur'an*. London: SPCK, 1911.

St. Clair-Tisdall, W. *The Sources of Islam*. Edinburgh: T. & T. Clark, 1901.

Stanton, H. U. W. *The Teaching of the Qur'an*. London: SPCK, 1919.

Thomas, Robert W. *Islam: Aspects and Prospects.* Villach: Light of Life, nd.

Trimingham, J. S. *Christianity among the Arabs in Pre-Islamic Times.* Beirut: Librairie du Liban, 1979.

Watt, W. Montgomery *Muhammad at Mecca.* Oxford: Oxford at the Clarendon Press, 1953, p. 159.

Webb, Peter 'Arab Origins: Identity, History and Islam', *British Academy Blog*, 20 July, 2015, https://www.britac.ac.uk/blog/arab-origins-identity-history-and-islam.

Zeitlin, Irving M. *The Historical Muhammad.* Oxford: Polity, 2017.

Zwemer, S. M. *The Moslem Doctrine of God.* New York: American Tract Society, 1905.

Notes

1   Richard Bell, *The Origin of Islam and its Christian Environment*. London: Frank Cass and Co Ltd, 1968, p. 1.

2   William Muir, *The Life of Mahomet from Original Sources*. London: Smith, Elder & Co, 1877, p. 208, fn. 1.

3   De Lacy O'Leary, *Arabia before Muhammad*. London: Routledge, 1927, repr. 2000, p. 23.

4   H. U. W. Stanton, *The Teaching of the Qur'an*. London: SPCK, 1919, p. 24.

5   J. S. Trimingham, *Christianity among the Arabs in Pre-Islamic Times*. Beirut: Librairie du Liban, 1979, pp. 308-10.

6   David Bukay, *From Muhammad to Bin Laden*. New Brunswick: Transaction Publishers, 2008, p. 38, fn. 9.

7   W. St Clair-Tisdall, *The Original Sources of the Qur'an*. London: SPCK, 1911, p. 34.

8   Francis E. Peters, *Muhammad and the Origin of Islam*. New York: New York State University Press, 1994, p. 122.

9   Ariel David, 'Before Islam: When Saudi Arabia was a
    Jewish Kingdom', *Haaretz*, 29 November 2017,
    https://www.haaretz.com/jewish/archaeology/1.709010.

10 Ghada Osman, 'Pre-Islamic Arab Converts to Christianity
    in Mecca and Medina', *The Muslim World*, Volume 95, 2005,
    p. 67.

11 Ghada Osman, p. 74.

12 Ghada Osman, p. 68.

13 J. S. Trimingham, pp. 308-310.

14 Joseph Azzi, *The Priest & the Prophet: the Christian Priest,
    Waraqa ibn Nawfal's profound Influence upon Muhammad*. Los
    Angeles: The Pen Publishers, 2005, p. 23.

15 J. D. Douglas and M. C. Tenney, *Zondervan Illustrated Bible
    Dictionary*. Grand Rapids: Zondervan, 2011, p. 1260.

16 Patricia Crone, *Hagarism*. Cambridge: CUP, 1977, p. 164.

17 W. St. Clair-Tisdall, *The Sources of Islam*. Edinburgh: T. & T.
    Clark, 1901, pp. 45, (14).

18 St. Clair-Tisdall, p. 6.

19 Joseph Azzi, *The Priest & the Prophet*, p. 3.

20 Zakaria Bashier, *The Makkan Crucible*. Leicester: The Islamic
    Foundation, 1991, p. 46.

21 Joseph Azzi, pp. 18-19.

22 A. Kuenen, *The Hibbert Lectures 1882: National Religions and
    Universal Religions: Lectures*. London: Williams and Norgate,
    1882, p. 19.

23 Fred M. Donner, *Muhammad and the Believers at the Origins of
    Islam*. Cambridge, Mass.: Harvard University Press, 2010, p.
    218.

24 Peter Webb, 'Arab Origins: Identity, History and Islam',
    British Academy, 20 July 2015, http://blog.britac.ac.uk/arab-
    origins-identity-history-and-islam/.

25 Fred M. Donner, *Muhammad and the Believers at the Origins of Islam*, p. 219.

26 Peter Webb, 'Arab Origins: Identity, History and Islam'.

27 Irving M. Zeitlin, *The Historical Muhammad*. Oxford: Polity, 2017, p. 50.

28 K. Cragg, *The Event of the Qur'an*. London: George Allen & Unwin Ltd, 1971, p. 54.

29 J. S. Trimingham, p. 311.

30 J. S. Trimingham, pp. 3-10.

31 H. A. R. Gibb, *Mohammedanism: An Historical Survey*. New York: OUP, 1962, p. 25.

32 *Muwatta* by Imam Malik cited in John Gilchrist, *Muhammad and the Religion of Islam*. Benoni, 1986, pp. 139-141, also at http://answering-islam.org/Gilchrist/Vol1/4a.html.

33 Gordon D. Newby, *A Concise Encyclopedia of Islam*. Oxford: Oneworld, 2002, p. 183.

34 'Amen' in Alison Latham (ed.), *The Oxford Companion to Music*. Oxford: OUP, 2002, p. 29.

35 D.S. Margoliouth, *Mohammed and the Rise of Islam*. London: G. P. Putnam's Sons, 1927, p. 106.

36 Barbara Roggema, 'A Christian Reading of the Qur'an: The Legend of Sergius-Bahira and its use of Qur'an and Sira' in David Thomas (ed.), *Syrian Christians under Islam: The First Thousand Years*. Leiden: Brill, 2001, p. 57.

37 Barbara Roggema, p. 64.

38 Barbara Roggema, p. 63.

39 Barbara Roggema, p. 61.

40 St. Clair-Tisdall, p. 66f.

41 St. Clair-Tisdall, p. 79.

42 Abraham Geiger, *Judaism and Islam*. 1898, repr. New York: KTAV, 1970, p. 80.

43 St. Clair-Tisdall, p. 64.

44 A. Guillaume, *The Life of Muhammad: A Translation of Ibn Ishaq's Sirat Rasul Allah*. Karachi: OUP, 1998, p. 139.

45 John Gilchrist, *Muhammad: The Prophet of Islam*, p. 207.

46 J. M. S. Baljon, *Modern Muslim Koran Interpretation (1880-1960)*. Leiden: Brill, 1961, pp. 38-39.

47 W. Montgomery Watt, *Muhammad at Mecca*. Oxford: Oxford at the Clarendon Press, 1953, p. 159.

48 John Bagot Glubb, *The Life and Times of Muhammad*. London: The History Book Club, 1970, p. 295.

49 A. Yusuf 'Ali, *The Holy Qur'an*. Leicester: The Islamic Foundation, 1975, p. 131, fn. 375.

50 St. Clair-Tisdall, p. 53.

51 D.S. Margoliouth, p. 61.

52 St. Clair-Tisdall, pp. 49-50.

53 St. Clair-Tisdall, p. 33.

54 John Gilchrist, *Muhammad and the Religion of Islam*. p. 201, also at http://answering-islam.org/Gilchrist/Vol1/5b.html.

55 A. Guillaume, *Islam*. London: Penguin, 1954, 1990, p. 62.

56 William Muir, *The Life of Mahomet from Original Sources*. London: Smith Elder & Co., 1877, p. 208, fn. 1.

57 Mustafa Ashour, *The Jinn: In the Qur'an and Sunna*. London. Dar Al-Taqwa, 1989, p. 16.

58 Bill Musk, *The Unseen Face of Islam*. London: Monarch Books, 2003, p. 47.

59 Imtiaz Yusuf, 'Laylat al-Qadr' in J. P. Esposito, *The Oxford Encyclopaedia of the Islamic World*. Oxford: OUP, 2009, p. 418.

60 Najah Bazzy, *The Beauty of Ramadan: A Guide to the Muslim Month of Prayer and Fasting*. Canton, Michigan: Read the Spirit Books, 2008, p. 39.

61 *Sura* 4:171 in George Sale (trans.), *The Koran: commonly called the Alkoran of Mohammed*. London: Frederick Warne and Co., nd., p. 72.

62 *Sura* 5:72-73 in Marmaduke Pickthall (trans.), *The Meaning of the Glorious Koran*. London: Everyman Publishers Plc, 1992, pp. 128-129.

63 *Sura* 5:77-79 in E H Palmer (trans.) *The Qur'an: The Sacred Books of the East: Vol VI, Part I*. 1880, repr. Delhi: Low Price Publications, 2006, p. 108.

64 *Sura* 5:116 in J M Rodwell (trans.), *The Koran*. 1909 repr. London: Everyman's Library, 1968, p. 499.

65 *Sura* 7:23 in M H Shakir (trans.), *Holy Qur'an*. Elmhurst, NY: Tahrike Tarsile Qur'an, Inc., p. 138.

66 Thomas Schirrmacher, *The Bible and the Koran*. Eugene, OR: Wipf & Stock, 2018, p. 67.

67 Parrinder, p. 40.

68 M. 'Ali, *Translation and Commentary on The Holy* Qur'an. 4th edition, Lahore, 1951, p. 40.

69 Geoffrey Parrinder, *Jesus in the Qur'an*. London: Sheldon Press, 1965, p. 26.

70 *Sura* 19:35-36 in Richard Bell, *The Qur'an: Volume I*. Edinburgh: T & T Clark, 1937, p. 287.

71 A. Yusuf 'Ali, *The Holy Qur'an*. Leicester: The Islamic Foundation, 1975, p. 236, fn. 663.

72 Parrinder, p. 109.

73 Gabriel Said Reynolds, 'The Muslim Jesus: Dead or Alive?', *Bulletin of SOAS*, Volume 72, No 2, 2009, p. 241.

74 *Sunan Abu Dawood*, 2025, at http://www.alim.org/library/hadith/SAD/2025.

75 Jonathan Benthall, *Islamic Charities and Islamic Humanism in Troubled Times*. Manchester: MUP, 2016, p. 173.

76 See *sura* 30:30; A. Yusuf 'Ali, *The Meaning of the Holy Qur'an*. Beltsville: Amana Publications, 1999, p. 1016, fn. 3541.

77 Yasien Mohamed, *Human Nature in Islam*. Kuala Lumpur: A. S. Noordeen, 1998, p. 41.

78 S. M. Zwemer, *The Moslem Doctrine of God*. New York: American Tract Society, 1905, p. 49.

79 Al-Bukhari, *Sahih al-Bukhari*, in *Alim*, at http://www.alim .org/library/hadith/SHB/16/4, Hadith 4:16.

80 *Sura* 16:31; A. Yusuf 'Ali, *The Meaning of the Holy Qur'an*. 1999, p. 644.

81 Yahiya Emerick, *The Complete Idiot's Guide to Understanding Islam*. Indianapolis: Alpha, 2003, p. 70.

82 'Shahid', in *Encyclopaedia of Islam*. Leiden: Brill, 1997, Vol 9, p. 204.

83 Al-Bukhari, *Sahih Bukhari* in *Alim*. Silver Spring: Maryland: ISL Software Corp., 1986-1999, now online at http://www.alim.org/library/hadith/SHB/301/1, Hadith 1:301.